PORTUGUESE PHRASEBOOK & DICTIONARY

Published by Collins
An imprint of HarperCollins Publishers
Westerhill Road
Bishopbriggs
Glasgow G64 2QT

HarperCollinsPublishers
1st Floor, Watermarque Building,
Ringsend Road, Dublin 4, Ireland

Fourth Edition 2016

10 9 8 7 6

ISBN 978-0-00-813593-5

www.collinsdictionary.com

Typeset by Davidson Publishing Solutions, Glasgow

Printed and bound in India by Replika Press Pvt. Ltd.

A catalogue record for this book is available from the British Library.

If you would like to comment on any aspect of this book, please contact us at the given address or online.
E-mail: dictionaries@harpercollins.co.uk
facebook.com/collinsdictionary
@collinsdict

Acknowledgements
We would like to thank those authors and publishers who kindly gave permission for copyright material to be used in the Collins Corpus. We would also like to thank Times Newspapers Ltd for providing valuable data.

Front cover image: Gare do Oriente railway station in Lisbon.
©anderm / Shutterstock.com

Using your phrasebook

Whether you're on holiday or on business, your **Collins Gem Phrasebook and Dictionary** is designed to help you locate the exact phrase you need, when you need it. You'll also gain the confidence to go beyond what is in the book, as you can adapt the phrases by using the dictionary section to substitute your own words.

The **Gem Phrasebook and Dictionary** includes:

- Over 60 topics arranged thematically, so that you can easily find an expression to suit the situation
- Simple pronunciation which accompanies each word and phrase, to make sure you are understood when speaking aloud
- Tips to safeguard against any cultural faux pas, providing the essential dos and don'ts of local customs or etiquette
- A basic grammar section which will help you to build on your phrases
- **FACE TO FACE** dialogue sections to give you a flavour of what to expect from a real conversation
- A handy map of the country which shows the major cities and how to pronounce them
- **YOU MAY HEAR** sections for common announcements and messages, so that you don't miss important information when out and about

- A user-friendly 3000 word dictionary to ensure you'll never be stuck for something to say
- **LIFELINE** phrases are listed on the inside covers for quick reference. These basic words and phrases will be essential to your time abroad

Before you jet off, it's worth spending time looking through the topics to see what is covered and becoming familiar with pronunciation.

The colour key below shows you how to search the phrasebook by theme, so you'll be able to find relevant phrases very quickly.

Talking to people
Getting around
Staying somewhere
Shopping
Leisure
Communications
Practicalities
Health
Eating out
Menu reader
Reference
Grammar
Dictionary

Contents

Pronouncing Portuguese

Portuguese is much easier to read than to speak. However, the pronunciation guide used in this book gives as accurate a guide as possible to the sounds of the language. The syllable to be stressed is printed in **bold**. Note that in conversation words tend to run together.

Vowels (a, e, i, o, u)

vowel	example	pronunciation	sounds like
a	saco	**sah**-koo	as in father
	fama	**fum**uh	hum
	fica	**fee**kuh	about
e	terra	**terr**-uh	terror
	enorme	eh-**norm**	enquire
	especial	eesh-pess**yahl**	happy
	de	duh	about
i	fica	**fee**kuh	police
	médico	**med**eekoo	happy
o	cobra	**koh**-bruh	all
	homem	**om**ayñ	au pair
	vaso	**vah**-zoo	boot
u	luvas	**loo**vush	boot

Notes:
The article **a** sounds like uh (as in the), unless stressed, i.e. **à** (ah).

e can sound like ay, e.g. **fecho** (**fay**shoo), but tends to be silent at the end of words, e.g. **pode** (pod) unless stressed, e.g. **bebé** (be-**be**). The word **e** (meaning and) always sounds like ee.

The article **o** and the letter **o** at the end of words always sound like oo.

Vowel combinations

ai	**mais**	mysh
ei	**peixe**	paysh
oi	**coisa**	**koy**-zuh
ou	**outro**	**oh**-troo

Nasal vowels

Vowels with a **tilde** ~ or followed by **m** or **n** in the same syllable should be pronounced nasally (letting air out through the nose as well as the mouth), as in French. We have represented this sound in the pronunciation by ñ, e.g.

tem = tayñ	**com** = koñ	**um** = ooñ
pão = powñ	**manhã** = mun-**yañ**	**põe** = poyñ

Other letters

	example	pronunciation	sounds like
ç	**serviço**	ser**vee**soo	
ch	**chá**	shah	
g	**gelo**	**zhay**-loo	as in measure
h			always silent
j	**loja**	**lozh**uh	as in measure
lh	**mulher**	mool-**yehr**	
nh	**tenho**	**ten**-yoo	
r/rr		always rolled; 'r' at beginning of word and double 'rr' are forceful and guttural (similar to French 'r')	
	(between vowels) **coisa**	**koy**-zuh	
s	(after vowel and at end of word)		
	está **lápis**	shta **lah**-peesh	
x	**caixa**	**ky**-shuh	
z	(at end of word) **faz**	fash	

Top ten tips

1. Use the formal form of address until you are asked to use the familiar form. Wait until you are invited to use first names.
2. There is no official religion, but the population predominantly identifies as Roman Catholic, this being stronger in the north than in the south.
3. It is a legal requirement in Portugal that everyone carries photographic proof of identity at all times.
4. Portuguese people are very proud of their culture, which is different from that of Spain!
5. To hire a car you often have to be at least 21, depending on the car hire company and on the vehicle. Often your driving licence must have been issued at least one year before, and if you are under 25 there may be an extra fee to pay.
6. Portuguese people have a sweet tooth; try some of their specialities such as **Toucinho do Céu** (heaven's bacon) and **Barriga de Freira** (nun's belly).
7. Most shopping centres are open 7 days a week from 10 a.m. to 11 p.m. or in some cases until midnight.
8. There are more than one thousand recipes to cook cod; one of the most famous is **Bacalhau à Brás**.
9. In restaurants, you have to ask for the bill; it's considered impolite of the waiter to bring the bill if you haven't asked for it.
10. Bars and restaurants tend to close on Sundays, except in busy areas such as Lisbon and the Algarve.

Talking to people

Hello/goodbye, yes/no

You will find that Portuguese people are quite formal and will appreciate it if you take the same approach to them as they take towards you.

Please	**Por favor/Faz favor** poor fuh-**vor**/fash fuh-**vor**
Thank you	**Obrigado(a)** oh-bree**gah**-doo(-duh)
Thanks very much	**Muito obrigado(a)** **mweeñ**to oh-bree**gah**-doo(-duh)
You're welcome!	**De nada!** duh **nah**-duh!
Yes	**Sim** seeñ
No	**Não** nowñ
OK	**Está bem** shta bayñ
Sir/Mr	**Senhor/Sr.** sun-**yor**

Madam/Mrs/Ms	**Senhora/Sra.** sun-**yo**ruh
Miss	**Menina** muh-**nee**nuh
Hello/Hi	**Olá** oh-**lah**
Goodbye/Bye	**Adeus** a**day**-oosh
See you later	**Até logo** uh-**te log**oo
See you tomorrow	**Até amanhã** uh-**te** amun-**yañ**
Good morning	**Bom dia** boñ **dee**-uh
Good afternoon/ evening	**Boa tarde** **boh**-uh tard
Goodnight	**Boa noite** **boh**-uh noyt
Excuse me! (to catch attention)	**Por favor!** poor fuh-**vor**!
Sorry!	**Desculpe!** dush**koolp**!
How are you?	**Como está?** **koh**-moo shta?
Fine, thanks	**Bem, obrigado(a)** bayñ, oh-bree**gah**-doo(-duh)
And you?	**E você?** ee voh-**say**?

I don't understand	**Não compreendo** nowñ koñpree-**en**doo
Do you speak English?	**Fala inglês?** **fah**-luh eeñ**glaysh**?

Key phrases

The easiest way to ask for something is by naming what you want and adding **por favor** (poor fuh-**vor**).

the (masculine)	**o/os** oo/oosh
glass/glasses	**o copo/os copos** oo **kop**oo/oosh **kop**oosh
a/one glass	**um copo** ooñ **kop**oo
the (feminine)	**a/as** uh/ush
key/keys	**a chave/as chaves** uh shahv/ush **shah**-vush
a/one key	**uma chave** **oo**muh shahv
my (masculine)	**o meu** oo **may**oo
(feminine)	**a minha** uh **meen**-yuh
my glass	**o meu copo** oo **may**oo **ko**poo

Talking to people

my key	**a minha chave** uh **meen**-yuh shahv
his/her/its/your	**o seu/a sua** oo **say**oo/uh **soo**-uh
his/her/its/your glass	**o seu copo** oo **say**oo **kop**oo
his/her/its/your key	**a sua chave** uh **soo**-uh shahv
Do you have...?	**Tem...?** tayñ...?
Do you have a room?	**Tem um quarto?** tayñ ooñ **kwar**too?
Do you have any milk?	**Tem leite?** tayñ layt?
Do you have stamps?	**Tem selos?** tayñ **sel**oosh?
I'd like...	**Queria...** **kree**-uh...
I'd like an ice cream	**Queria um gelado** **kree**-uh ooñ zhuh-**lah**-doo
I'd like to book a table	**Queria reservar uma mesa** **kree**-uh ruh-zer**var oo**muh **may**-zuh
I'd like pasta	**Queria massa** **kree**-uh **mass**uh
We'd like...	**Queríamos...** **kree**-uhmoosh...
We'd like two cakes	**Queríamos dois bolos** **kree**-uhmoosh doysh **boh**loosh

More...	**Mais...** mysh...
More bread	**Mais pão** mysh powñ
More water	**Mais água** mysh **ahg**-wuh
Another...	**Outro(a)...** **oh**-troo(truh)...
Another milky coffee	**Outro galão** **oh**-troo ga**lowñ**
Another lager	**Outra cerveja** **oh**-truh ser**vay**-zhuh
How much is it?	**Quanto é?** **kwuñ**too e?
How much does it cost?	**Quanto custa?** **kwuñ**too **koosh**tuh?
large	**grande** gruñd
small	**pequeno** puh-**kay**noo
with	**com** koñ
without	**sem** sayñ
Where is...?	**Onde é...?** **on**duh e...?
Where are...?	**Onde são/estão...?** **on**duh sowñ/shtowñ...?

Where is the toilet?	**Onde é a casa de banho?** **on**duh e uh **kah**-zuh duh **bun**-yoo?
Where are the children?	**Onde estão as crianças?** **on**duh shtowñ ush kree-**uñ**sush?
How do I get...?	**Como se vai...?** **koh**-moo suh vy...?
to the station	**para a estação** **pa**ruh a shtuh-**sowñ**
to the centre	**ao centro** ow **sen**troo
There is/are...	**Há...** a...
There isn't/ aren't any...	**Não há...** nowñ a...
When...?	**Quando...?** **kwuñ**doo...?
At what time is...?	**A que horas é...?** uh kee **or**uhsh e...?
today	**hoje** ohzh
tomorrow	**amanhã** amun-**yañ**
Can I...?	**Posso...?** **poss**oo...?
Can I smoke?	**Posso fumar?** **poss**oo foo**mar**?
Can I pay?	**Posso pagar?** **poss**oo puh-**gar**?

How does this work?	**Como funciona?** **koh**-moo foonss-**yo**nuh?
What does this mean?	**Que quer dizer isto?** kuh kayr dee**zehr eesh**too?

Signs and notices

homens	gentlemen
senhoras	ladies
aberto	open
fechado	closed
água para beber/ água potável	drinking water
primeiros socorros	first aid
cheio/lotado	full
liquidação total	closing-down sale
caixa	cash desk
empurre	push
puxe	pull
lavabos/sanitários	toilets
livre	vacant/free
ocupado	engaged/occupied
não funciona	out of order
avariado	out of order

para alugar	for hire/rent
para venda	for sale
saldos	sales
cave	basement
rés do chão	ground floor
entrada	entrance
bilheteira	ticket office
equitação	horse riding
vagas/vago	vacancies/vacant
banheiro	lifeguard (beach)
casas de banho	bathrooms
degustação	tasting
pagar na caixa	pay at cash desk
depósito de bagagens	left luggage
quente	hot
proibido	forbidden/no...
não mexer/não tocar	do not touch
completo	no vacancies
vestiários	changing rooms
impedido	engaged
descontos	reductions
informações	information
perigo	danger
fumadores	smoking

Polite expressions

There are three forms of address in Portuguese: formal (**o senhor/a senhora**), semi-formal (**você** – for both sexes) and informal (**tu** – for both sexes). Always stick to the formal when addressing older people, or the semi-formal for people of your own age and status, until you are invited to use the informal **tu**.

The meal was delicious	**A refeição estava deliciosa** uh ruhfay-**sowñ shtah**vuh duhlees-**yoh**zuh
Thank you very much	**Muito obrigado(a)** **mweeñ**too oh-bree**gah**-doo(-duh)
This is a gift for you	**Isto é um presente para si** **eesh**too e ooñ pruh-**zeñt pa**ruh see
Pleased to meet you	**Muito prazer** **mweeñ**too pruh-**zehr**
This is my husband	**Este é o meu marido** esht e oo **may**oo muh**ree**doo
This is my wife	**Esta é a minha mulher** **esh**tuh e uh **meen**-yuh mool-**yehr**
Enjoy your holiday!	**Boas férias!** **boh**-ush **fehr**-yush!

Celebrations

Merry Christmas!	**Bom Natal!** boñ nuh-**tahl**!
Happy New Year!	**Feliz Ano Novo!** fuh-**leesh ah**-noo **noh**-voo!
Happy birthday!	**Feliz aniversário!** fuh-**leesh** aneever-**sar**-yoo!
Have a good trip!	**Muito boa viagem!** **mweeñ**too **boh**-uh vee-**ah**-zhayñ!

Making friends

In this section we have used the familiar form **tu** for the questions. **Tu** is widely used between young people soon after being introduced, and between close friends and relatives of any age.

FACE TO FACE

Como te chamas?
koh-moo tuh **shah**-mush?
What's your name?

Chamo-me...
shah-moo-muh...
My name is...

De onde és?
duh **oñ**duh esh?
Where are you from?

Sou inglês/inglesa
soh eeñ**glaysh**/eeñ**glay**zuh
I'm English (masc./fem.)

Muito prazer
mweeñto pruh-**zehr**
Pleased to meet you

How old are you?	**Quantos anos tens?** **kwuñ**toosh **ah**-noosh tayñsh?
I'm ... years old	**Tenho ... anos** **ten**-yoo ... **ah**-noosh
Where do you live?	**Onde vives?** **oñ**duh **vee**vush?
Where do you live? (plural)	**Onde vivem?** **oñ**duh vee**vayñ**?
I live in London	**Vivo em Londres** **vee**-voo ayñ **loñ**drush
I'm still studying	**Sou estudante** soh shtoo**duñt**
I work	**Trabalho** truh-**bahl**-yoo
I'm retired	**Sou reformado(a)** soh refoor**mah**-doo(uh)
I'm...	**Sou...** soh...

England/ English	**Inglaterra/inglês (inglesa)** eeñ-gluh-**terr**-uh/eeñ**glaysh** (eeñ**glayz**uh)
Scotland/ Scottish	**Escócia/escocês (escocesa)** eesh-**koss**-yuh/eesh-ko**saysh** (eesh-ko**say**-zuh)
Wales/Welsh	**Gales/galês (galesa)** **gal**eesh/ga**laysh** (ga**lay**zuh)
Ireland/Irish	**Irlanda/irlandês (irlandesa)** eer**luñ**duh/eerluñ**daysh** (eerluñ**day**-zuh)
USA/American	**América/americano(a)** uh**meh**reekuh/uhmehree**kuh**noo (uh)
Australia/ Australian	**Austrália/australiano(a)** owst**rah**leeya/owstrahlee**yah**noo (uh)
single	**solteiro(a)** sol**tay**-roo(uh)
married	**casado(a)** ka**zah**-doo(uh)
divorced	**divorciado(a)** deevoors-**yah**-doo(uh)
I have...	**Tenho...** **ten**-yoo...
a boyfriend	**namorado** nuh-moo-**rah**-doo
a girlfriend	**namorada** nuh-moo-**rah**-duh

a partner	**companheiro(a)** koñpun-**yay**-roo(uh)
I have ... children	**Tenho ... filhos** **ten**-yoo ... **feel**-yoosh
I have no children	**Não tenho filhos** nowñ **ten**-yoo **feel**-yoosh
I'm here...	**Estou aqui...** shtoh uh-**kee**...
on holiday	**de férias** duh **fehr**-yush
for work	**por motivo de trabalho** poor moo**tee**-voo duh truh-**bahl**-yoo

Work

What work do you do?	**Em que trabalhas?** ayñ kuh truh-**bahl**-yuhsh?
I'm...	**Sou...** soh...
a doctor	**médico(a)** **med**eekoo(uh)
a teacher	**professor(a)** proofuh-**sor**(uh)
I work in...	**Trabalho em...** truh-**bahl**-yoo ayñ...

a shop	**numa loja** **oo**muh **lozh**uh
a factory	**numa fábrica** **oo**muh **fahb**reekuh
a bank	**num banco** ooñ **buñ**koo
I'm self-employed	**Trabalho por conta própria** truh-**bahl**-yoo poor **koñ**-tuh **pro**pree-uh

Weather

aguaceiros ugwuh-**say**roosh	showers
limpo **leeñ**poo	clear
a chuva uh **shoo**vuh	rain
nublado noo**blah**-doo	cloudy

It's sunny	**Faz sol** fash sol
It's raining	**Está a chover** shta uh shoo**vehr**
It's windy	**Está vento** shta **veñ**too
What a lovely day!	**Que lindo dia!** kuh **leeñ**doo **dee**-uh!

What awful weather!	**Que mau tempo!** kuh mow **teñ**poo!
It's very hot/cold	**Está muito calor/frio** shta **mweeñ**to ka**lor**/**free**-oo
What is the temperature?	**Qual é a temperatura?** kwal e uh teñpra**too**ruh?

Getting around

Asking the way

em frente ayñ freñt	opposite
ao lado de ow **lah**-doo duh	next to
perto de **pehr**too duh	near to
o semáforo oo suh-**maf**ooroo	traffic lights
na esquina nuh **shkee**nuh	at the corner

FACE TO FACE

Por favor, senhor/senhora! Como se vai à estação?
poor fuh-**vor**, sun-**yor**/sun-**yor**uh! **koh**-moo suh vy a shtuh-**sowñ**?
Excuse me, sir/madam! How do I/we get to the station?

Siga em frente até a igreja e depois vire à esquerda/direita
see-guh ayñ freñt uh-**te** uh ee-**greh**zhuh ee duh-**poysh vee**ree a eesh-**ker**duh/dee-**ray**tuh
Keep straight on up to the church and then turn left/right

É longe? e loñzh? Is it far?	
Não, duzentos metros/cinco minutos nowñ, doo-**zeñ**toosh **met**roosh/**seeñ**koo mee-**noo**toosh No, 200 metres/5 minutes	
Obrigado(a)! oh-bree**gah**-doo(-duh)! Thanks!	

We're lost	**Estamos perdidos** **shtah**-moosh per**dee**-doosh
Is this the right way to...?	**É este o caminho para...?** e esht oo kuh-**meen**-yoo **pa**ruh...?
Can you show me where it is on the map?	**Pode-me mostrar no mapa?** **pod**-muh moosh-**trar** noo **mah**-puh?

YOU MAY HEAR...

Depois de passar a ponte de**poysh** duh puh-**sar** uh poñt	After passing the bridge
lá lah	over there
ali/aqui a**lee**/uh-**kee**	there/here

Bus and coach

FACE TO FACE

Por favor, senhor/senhora! Que autocarro vai ao centro da cidade?
poor fuh-**vor**, sun-**yor**/sun-**yor**uh! kuh owtoo-**karr**oo vy ow **señ**troo duh see**dahd**?
Excuse me, sir/madam! Which bus goes to the city centre?

Número 15
noomeroo **keeñ**zuh
Number 15

Onde apanho o autocarro?
oñduh uh-**pahn**-yoo oo owtoo-**karr**oo?
Where do I catch the bus?

Ali, em frente da farmácia
a**lee**, ayñ freñt duh far**mass**-yuh
There, in front of the pharmacy

Is there a bus to...?	**Há autocarro para...?** a owtoo-**karr**oo **pa**ruh...?
to the centre	**para o centro** **pa**ruh oo **señ**troo
to the beach	**para a praia** **pa**ruh uh **pry**-uh
A child's ticket	**Um bilhete para criança** ooñ beel-**yet** **par**uh kree-**uñ**suh

When is the first/the last bus to...?	**A que horas é o primeiro/ o último autocarro para...?** uh kee **or**uz e oo pree**may**-roo/ oo **ool**teemoo owtoo-**karr**oo **pa**ruh...?
Please tell me when to get off	**Pode-me dizer quando devo sair?** **pod**-muh dee**zehr** **kwuñ**doo **deh**-voo sah-**eer**?
coach	**a camioneta** kuh-mee-oh **neh**tuh
shuttle bus	**o autocarro shuttle** owtoo-**karr**oo shuttle

YOU MAY HEAR...	
Este autocarro não para em... aysht owtoo-**karr**oo nowñ **pah**-ruh ayñ...	This bus doesn't stop in...
Tem que apanhar o... tayñ kuh apun-**yar** oo...	You must catch the...

Metro

There are now four metro systems in Portugal: Lisbon, Porto, Almada (across the river Tagus) and Mirandela (in the North). Mirandela and Almada are both overground networks. You can buy a monthly season ticket with an ID photo (**um passe**) or a **cartão viva viagem** which you can top up. These cards allow you to travel on both metro and bus services.

entrada ehñ**trah**-duh	entrance
saída sah-**ee**duh	way out/exit
a linha de metro uh **leen**-yuh duh **met**roo	metro line

Where is the nearest metro station?	**Onde é a estação de metro mais próxima?** **oñ**duh e uh shtuh-**sowñ** duh **met**roo mysh **pross**eemuh?
How does the ticket machine work?	**Como funciona a máquina automática?** **koh**-moo foonss-**yo**nuh uh **mak**eenuh owtoo**mah**-teekuh?
Do you have a map of the metro?	**Tem um mapa do metro?** tayñ ooñ **mah**-puh doo **met**roo?
Do I have to change?	**Tenho que mudar?** **ten**-yoo kuh moo**dar**?
Which line is it for...?	**Qual é a linha para...?** kwal e uh **leen**-yuh **pa**ruh...?
What is the next stop?	**Qual é a próxima paragem?** kwal e uh **pross**eemuh puh-**rah**-zhayñ?

Train

There are two types of train ticket for all trains: **conforto** (1st class) and **turística** (2nd class). On longer trips, where it is advisable to book ahead (**reservar lugares**), you can book online. The **Alfa Pendular** is a fast, intercity train and the most expensive. The **Intercidades** is a fast, long-distance service, and the medium-distance **Inter-Regional** stops at all the main stations.

a estação uh shtuh-**sowñ**	station
partidas par**tee**dush	departures
chegadas shuh-**gah**-dush	arrivals
o bilhete online beel-**yet** online	e-ticket
a reserva online ruh**zehr**vuh online	e-booking

Where is the station?	**Onde é a estação?** **oñ**duh e uh shtuh-**sowñ**?
First/Second class	**Primeira/Segunda classe** pree**may**ruh/se**goon**duh klass
I booked online	**Fiz a reserva online** feezh uh ruh**zeh**rvuh online

Getting around

I want to book a seat on the Alfa to Aveiro	**Queria reservar um lugar no Alfa para Aveiro** **kree**-uh ruh-zer**var** ooñ loo**gar** noo **ahl**fuh **pa**ruh a**vay**roo
When does it arrive in...?	**A que horas chega a...?** uh kee **or**ush **sheh**-guh uh...?
Do I have to change?	**Tenho que mudar?** **ten**-yoo kuh moo**dar**?
Where?	**Onde?** **oñ**duh?
Which platform does it leave from?	**De que plataforma parte?** duh kuh platuh**for**muh part?
Is this the train for...?	**É este o comboio para...?** e aysht oo koñ**boy**oo **pa**ruh...?
Does the train stop at...?	**O comboio para em...?** oo koñ**boy**oo **pah**-ruh ayñ...?
Is this (seat) free?	**Está livre?** shta **lee**vruh?

FACE TO FACE

Quando é o próximo comboio para...?
kwuñdoo e oo **pross**eemoo koñ**boy**oo **pa**ruh...?
When is the next train to...?

Às 17.00
ash dezuh-**set**uh **or**ush
At 5 p.m.

Queria três bilhetes, por favor
kree-uh traysh beel-**yetsh** poor fuh-**vor**
I'd like three tickets, please

Só de ida ou ida e volta?
soh duh **ee**duh oh **ee**duh ee **vol**tuh?
Single or return?

Ida e volta, por favor
eeduh ee **vol**tuh poor fuh-**vor**
Return, please

Taxi

Taxis in Portugal have an illuminated **taxi** sign on top and are usually painted beige, but some older ones are still green and black. The driver's ID and the meter should both be displayed inside the car. There is a fixed tariff starting at €3.25, but increasing to €3.90 after 9 p.m., at weekends, and during holidays. Within the city you can get a standard fare, but outside the city limits you'll be charged per kilometre, and the driver is entitled to charge for the return fare. You'll also pay a surcharge if you are travelling with luggage. To ask for a receipt, say **Queria uma fatura, por favor**. It's a good idea to ask for this in advance, as you get in the car.

a praça de taxis uh **prah**-suh duh **tak**seesh	taxi rank

Where can I/ we get a taxi?	**Onde se pode arranjar um táxi?** **oñ**duh suh pod arruñ**zhar** ooñ **tak**see?
How much will it cost by taxi...?	**Quanto custa ir de táxi...?** **kwuñ**too **koosh**tuh eer duh **tak**see...?
to the centre	**ao centro** ow **señ**troo
to the station	**à estação** a shtuh-**sowñ**
to the airport	**ao aeroporto** ow uh-ayroo-**por**too
to this address	**a esta morada** uh **esh**tuh moo**rah**-duh
Please take me to...	**Por favor leve-me a...** poor fuh-**vor lev**-muh uh...
How much is it?	**Quanto é?** **kwuñ**too e?
Keep the change	**Guarde o troco** gward oo **tro**koo
Sorry, I don't have any change	**Desculpe, não tenho troco** dush**koolp**, nowñ **ten**-yoo **tro**koo
Is it far?	**É longe?** e loñzh?

Boat and ferry

a travessia uh truh-**vess**-yuh	crossing
o cruzeiro oo kroo**zay**roo	cruise
o camarote oo kumuh-**roht**	cabin

When is the next boat to...?	**Quando parte o próximo barco para...?** **kwuñ**doo part oo **pross**eemoo **bar**koo **pa**ruh...?
Is there a car ferry to...?	**Há um ferry-boat para...?** a ooñ ferry-boat **pa**ruh...?
How much is a ... ticket?	**Quanto é o bilhete...?** **kwuñ**too e oo beel-**yet**...?
single/return	**de ida/de ida e volta** **dee**duh/**dee**duh ee **vol**tuh
How much is the crossing for a car and ... people?	**Quanto é a passagem para ... pessoas e um carro?** **kwuñ**too e uh puh-**sah**-zhayñ **pa**ruh ... puh-**so**-ush ee ooñ **karr**oo?
How long is the journey?	**Quanto dura a viagem?** **kwuñ**to **doo**ruh vee-**ah**-zhayñ?
Where does the boat leave from?	**De onde parte o barco?** dee **oñ**duh part oo **bar**koo?

Air travel

The major airports in Portugal are **Lisboa** (Aeroporto da Portela), **Porto** (Aeroporto Francisco Sá Carneiro) and **Faro**, in the Algarve (Aeroporto de Faro).

How do I get to the airport?	**Como se vai para o aeroporto?** **koh**-moo suh vy **pa**ruh oo ayroo-**por**too?
To the airport, please	**Para o aeroporto, por favor** **pa**ruh oo ayroo-**por**too, poor fuh-**vor**
How long does it take to get to the airport?	**Quanto tempo leva a chegar ao aeroporto?** **kwuñ**too **teñ**poo **leh**-vuh uh shuh-**gar** ow uh-ayroo-**por**too?
Where do I check in for...(airline)?	**Onde faço o check-in para...?** **oñ**duh **fah**-soo oo check-in **pa**ruh...?
Where is the luggage for the flight from...?	**Onde está a bagagem do voo de...?** **oñ**duh shta uh buh-**gah**-zhayñ doo **voh**-oo duh...?
Where can I print my ticket?	**Onde posso imprimir o meu bilhete?** **o**ñduh possoo eempree**meer** oo **may**oo beel-**yet?**
I have my boarding pass on my smartphone	**Tenho o meu cartão de embarque no smartphone** **ten**-yoo oo **mayo** kar**towñ** duh ayñ-**bark noo smart**-fohn

checked luggage	**a bagagem de porão** buh-**gah**-zhayñ duh poo**rowñ**
hand luggage	**a bagagem de mão** buh-**gah**-zhayñ duh mown

YOU MAY HEAR...

O seu voo está atrasado oo **say**oo **voh**-oo shta atruh-**zah**-doo	Your flight is delayed
Proibido transportar líquidos proee-**bee**doo truñspoor-**tar lee**keedoosh	No liquids
A sua bagagem excede o limite de peso uh **soo**-uh buh-**gah**-zhayñ aysh-**sed** oo lee**meet** duh **peh**zoo	Your luggage exceeds the maximum weight

Customs control

With the Single European Market, EU citizens are subject only to highly selective spot checks and can go through the green customs channel (unless they have goods to declare).

UE oo ay	EU
bilhete de identidade beel-**yet** duh eedeñtee**dahd**	identity card

Do I have to pay duty on this?	**É preciso pagar direitos para isto?** e pre-**see**zoo puh-**gar** dee**ray**-toosh **pa**ruh **eesh**too?
It is for my own personal use	**É para uso pessoal** e **pa**ruh **oo**zoo puh-**swahl**
We are going to...	**Vamos a...** **vuh**-moosh uh...

Car hire

Car rental companies in Portugal normally have a minimum age for hiring a car (21, 23 or 25, depending on the company and type of vehicle). Some companies also have a maximum age limit of 75. A small number of companies will rent to drivers under 21, provided they pay a 'young driver' surcharge.

a carta de condução uh **kar**tuh duh koñdoo**sowñ**	driving licence
o seguro oo se**goo**roo	insurance
a marcha atrás uh **mar**shuh uh-**trash**	reverse gear

I'd like to hire a car	**Queria alugar um carro** **kree**-uh aloo**gar** ooñ **karr**oo
for ... days	**para ... dias** **pa**ruh ... **dee**-ush
for the weekend	**o fim de semana** oo feeñ duh suh-**mah**-nuh
What are your rates...?	**Quais são as tarifas...?** kwysh sowñ ush tuh-**ree**-fush...?
per day/ per week	**por dia/por semana** poor **dee**-uh/poor suh-**mah**-nuh
How much is the deposit?	**Quanto deixo de sinal?** **kwuñ**too **day**-shoo duh see**nahl**?
Is there a mileage (kilometre) charge?	**Paga-se quilometragem?** **pah**-guh-suh keelome**trah**-zhayñ?
Is fully comprehensive insurance included?	**Inclui o seguro contra todos os riscos?** eeñ-**klwee** oo se**goo**roo **koñ**truh **toh**-doosh oosh **reesh**koosh?
Do I have to return the car here?	**Tenho que devolver o carro aqui?** **ten**-yoo kuh duh-vol**vehr** oo **karr**oo uh-**kee**?
By what time?	**Até que horas?** uh-**te** kuh **or**ush?
I'd like to leave it in...	**Gostaria de o deixar em...** gooshtuh-**ree**-uh duh oo day**shar** ayñ...
What shall I do if the car breaks down?	**Que devo fazer se o carro se avariar?** kuh **deh**-voo fa**zehr** suh oo **karr**oo suh avaree**ar**?

YOU MAY HEAR...	
Por favor devolva o carro com o depósito cheio poor fuh-**vor** duh-**vol**vuh oo **karr**oo koñ oo duh-**poz**eetoo **shay**oo	Please return the car with a full tank

Driving

sem chumbo sayñ **shoom**boo	unleaded
gasóleo ga**zol**-yoo	diesel
a gasolina uh gazoo-**lee**nuh	petrol
a bomba de gasolina uh **boñ**buh duh gazoo-**lee**nuh	petrol pump/station

Can I/we park here?	**Pode-se estacionar aqui?** **pod**-suh shtass-yoo**nar** uh-**kee**?
Do I/we need a parking ticket?	**É preciso um bilhete?** e pre-**see**zoo ooñ beel-**yet**?
Fill it up, please	**Encha, por favor** **eñ**shuh, poor fuh-**vor**

Can you check the oil/the water?	**Pode ver o óleo/a água?** pod vehr oo **ol**-yoo/uh **ahg**-wuh?
Can you check the tyre pressure, please?	**Pode ver a pressão dos pneus, por favor?** pod vehr uh pruh**sowñ** doosh **pnay**-oosh, poor fuh-**vor**?

Breakdown

The Portuguese equivalent of the **AA** is **ACP** (**Automóvel Clube de Portugal**). **ACP** has partnerships with many foreign associations, so if your car breaks down, you should call your own country's roadside assistance company (e.g. the **AA**) and they will contact **ACP** to help you.

My car has broken down	**Tenho o carro avariado** **ten**-yoo oo **karr**oo avaree-**ah**-doo
The car won't start	**O carro não pega** oo **karr**oo nowñ **peh**-guh
I've run out of petrol	**Não tenho gasolina** nowñ **ten**-yoo gazoo-**lee**nuh
Is there a garage near here?	**Há alguma garagem por aqui?** a al**goo**muh ga**rah**-zhayñ poor uh-**kee**?
It's leaking...	**Está a perder...** shta uh per**dehr**...

petrol	**gasolina** gazoo-**lee**nuh
oil	**óleo** **ol**-yoo
water	**água** **ahg**-wuh

Car parts

The ... doesn't work	**O/A ... não funciona** oo/uh ... nowñ foonss-**yo**nuh
The ... don't work	**Os/As ... não funcionam** oosh/ush ... nowñ foonss-**yo**nowñ

accelerator	**o acelerador**	asseh-leruh-**dor**
battery	**a bateria**	batuh-**ree**-uh
bonnet	**o capot**	kah-**po**
brakes	**os travões**	tra-**voyñsh**
clutch	**a embraiagem**	ayñ-bry-**ah**-zhayñ
distributor	**o distribuidor**	deesh-tree-bwee-**dor**
engine	**o motor**	moo**tor**
exhaust pipe	**o tubo de escape**	**too**boo dush**kap**
fuse	**o fusível**	foo**zee**vel

gears	**as mudanças**	moo**duñ**sush
handbrake	**o travão de mão**	tra**vowñ** duh mowñ
headlights	**os faróis**	fa**roysh**
ignition	**a ignição**	eegnee-**sowñ**
indicator	**o indicador**	eeñdeekuh-**dor**
points	**os platinados**	platee-**nah**-doosh
radiator	**o radiador**	radee-uh-**dor**
rear lights	**os farolins traseiros**	fuhroo**liñsh** tra**zay**roosh
seat belt	**o cinto de segurança**	**seeñ**too duh segoo**ruñ**-suh
spare wheel	**a roda sobres-salente**	**rod**uh sobruh-sa**leñt**
spark plugs	**as velas**	**vel**ush
starter motor	**o motor de arranque**	moo**tor** duh a**rruñk**
steering	**a direção**	deere**sowñ**
steering wheel	**o volante**	voo**luñt**
tyre	**o pneu**	**pnay**-oo
wheel	**a roda**	**rod**uh
windscreen	**o para-brisas**	**pah**-ruh-**bree**zush
windscreen washer	**o lava para-brisas**	**lah**vuh **pah**-ruh-**bree**zush
windscreen wiper	**o limpa para-brisas**	**leeñ**puh **pah**-ruh-**bree**zush

Road signs

danger

customs

spaces

full

no parking

north

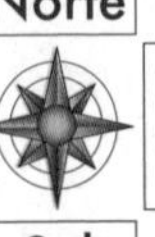

west

east

south

diversion

end of roadworks

speed limits are in kilometres per hour

toll station for motorway

on Wednesdays

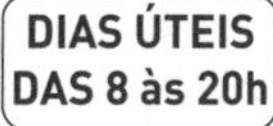

weekdays from 8 to 20h

DAS
6 às 15h

from 6 to 15h

Staying somewhere

Hotel (booking)

FACE TO FACE

Queria reservar um quarto para duas noites
kree-uh ruh-zer**var** ooñ **kwar**too **pa**ruh **doo**ush **noy**tsh
I'd like to book a room for two nights

Individual ou de casal?
eeñdeeveed-**wahl** oh duh kuh-**zahl**?
Single or double?

De casal com uma cama extra para criança, por favor
duh kuh-**zahl** koñ **oo**muh **kah**-muh **aysh**-truh **pa**ruh kree-**uñ**suh, poor fuh-**vor**
Double with an extra bed for a child, please

Qual é o preço por noite/por semana?
kwal e oo **pray**-soo poor noyt/poor suh-**mah**-nuh?
How much is it per night/per week?

with bath — **com casa de banho**
koñ **kah**-zuh duh **bun**-yoo

with shower — **com chuveiro**
koñ shoo-**vay**roo

with a double bed	**com cama de casal** koñ **kah**-muh duh kuh-**zahl**
with twin beds	**com duas camas** koñ **doo**-ush **kah**-mush
with a cot	**com um berço** koñ oon **behr**-soo
Is breakfast included?	**Inclui o pequeno-almoço?** eeñ-**klwee** oo puh-**kay**noo al**moh**-soo?
Do you have any bedrooms on the ground floor?	**Tem quartos no rés do chão?** tayñ alg**oonsh** **kwar**toosh noo resh doo **showñ**?
I'd like to see the room	**Queria ver o quarto** **kree**-uh vehr oo **kwar**too

YOU MAY HEAR...	
Não temos vagas nowñ **tay**moosh **vah**-gush	We've no vacancies
Estamos cheios **shtah**-moosh **shay**oosh	We're full up
Para quantas noites? **pa**ruh **kwuñ**tush noytsh?	For how many nights?
O seu nome, por favor? oo **say**oo nom, poor fuh-**vor**?	Your name, please?

Staying somewhere

Hotel desk

On arrival at a hotel, the receptionist will ask for your passport to register your stay. This is an official requirement and should not be misinterpreted.

I booked a room...	**Reservei um quarto...** ruh-zer**vay** ooñ **kwar**too...
in the name of...	**em nome de...** ayñ nom duh...
I reserved the room(s) online	**Reservei o(s) quarto(s) online** ruh-zer**vay** oo(sh) **kwar**toosh online
by phone	**por telefone** poor tuh-luh-**fon**
Is there a hotel restaurant or bar?	**O hotel tem restaurante ou bar?** oo oh-**tel** tayñ rushtoh-**ruñt** o bar?
Where can I park the car?	**Onde posso estacionar o carro?** **oñ**duh **poss**oo shtass-yoo**nar** oo **karr**oo?
Are there any toilets for disabled people?	**Há casas de banho especiais para deficientes?** a **kah**-zush duh **bun**-yoo shpuh-ssee-**ysh par**uh duh-feess-**yeñtsh**?
What time is...?	**A que hora é...?** uh kee **or**uh e...?
dinner	**o jantar** oo zhuñ**tar**

breakfast	**o pequeno-almoço** oo puh-**kay**noo al**moh**-soo
The key for room number...	**A chave do quarto número...** uh shahv doo **kwar**too **noo**meroo...
I'm leaving tomorrow	**Vou-me embora amanhã** **voh**-muh em**boh**-ruh amun-**yañ**
Where is the lift?	**Onde é o elevador?** **oñ**duh e oo eeluh-vuh-**dor?**

Camping

Have you places?	**Tem vagas?** tayñ **vah**-gush?
How much is it per night...?	**Quanto é por noite...?** **kwuñ**too e poor noyt...?
for a tent	**por tenda** poor **teñ**duh
per person	**por pessoa** poor puh-**so**-uh
Are showers included in the price?	**Os duches são incluídos no preço?** oosh **doosh**ush sowñ eeñ-**klwee**doosh noo **pray**-soo?
Is hot water/ electricity included in the price?	**A água quente/electricidade está incluído no preço?** uh **ahg**-wuh keñt/ eeletree-see**dahd** shta eeñ-**klwee**doo noo **pray**-soo?

Can we park the caravan/ trailer here?	**Podemos estacionar a caravana/roulotte aqui?** poo**deh**-moosh shtass-yoo**nar** uh karuh-**vah**-nuh/roo**lot** uh-**kee**?

Self-catering

If you arrive with no accommodation and want to go self-catering, look for signs saying **Aluguer de Apartamentos** (apartments for rent).

Who do we contact if there are problems?	**Quem podemos contactar em caso de problemas?** kayñ poo**deh**-moosh koñtak**tar** ayñ **kah**-zoo duh proo**bleh**-mush?
How does the heating work?	**Como funciona o aquecimento?** **koh**-moo foon**syo**nuh oo akuh-see**mayñ**too?
Is there always hot water?	**Há sempre água quente?** a **sayñ**pruh **ahg**-wuh keñt?
Where is the nearest supermarket?	**Onde é o supermercado mais perto?** **oñ**duh e oo sooper-mer**kah**-doo mysh **pehr**too?
recycling	**a reciclagem** ruhsee**kla**zhayñ

Shopping

Shopping phrases

Many shops still close for lunch between 1 and 3 p.m., but most now remain open throughout the day. Large department stores and food shops are generally open from 9 a.m. to 7 p.m., whereas shopping centres are open from 10 a.m. to 10 p.m.

FACE TO FACE

Que deseja?
kuh de**zay**zhuh?
Can I help you?

Um/uma..., por favor
ooñ/**oo**muh..., poor fuh-**vor**
A ..., please

Mais alguma coisa?
mysh al**goo**muh **koy**-zuh?
Would you like anything else?

Não, é tudo. Quanto é?
nowñ, e **too**doo. **kwuñ**too e?
No, that's all. How much is it?

Where is...?	**Onde é...?** **oñ**duh e...?
Do you have...?	**Tem...?** tayñ...?

Shops

saldo/descontos **sahl**doo/dush**koñ**toosh	sale/reductions
liquidação leekeeduh-**sowñ**	closing-down sale
hoje, aberto até às... ohzh, uh-**behr**too uh-**te** ush...	open today until...

baker's	**padaria**	puduh-**ree**-uh
bookshop	**livraria**	leevruh-**ree**-uh
butcher's	**talho**	**tahl**-yoo
cake shop	**pastelaria**	pushtuh-la**ree**-uh
clothes (women's)	**roupa de senhora**	**roh**-puh duh sun-**yor**uh
clothes (men's)	**roupa para homem**	**roh**-puh **pa**ruh **om**ayñ
gifts	**brindes**	**breeñ**-dush
glasses	**óculos**	**oh**-kooloosh

Shopping

greengrocer's	**frutaria**	frootuh-**ree**-uh
grocer's	**mercearia**	mersee-uh-**ree**-uh
hairdresser's	**cabeleireiro(a)**	kuh-buh-lay-**ray**-roo(-ruh)
jeweller's	**joalharia**	zhwal-yuh-**ree**-uh
market	**mercado**	mer**kah**-doo
optician	**oculista**	okoo**leesh**-tuh
pharmacy	**farmácia**	far**mass**-yuh
shoe shop	**sapataria**	sapuh-tuh-**ree**-uh
shop	**loja**	**lozh**uh
souvenir shop	**a loja de souvenirs**	**lozh**uh de sooveh**neersh**
stationer's	**papelaria**	papuh-la**ree**-uh
supermarket	**supermercado**	sooper-mer**kah**-doo
tobacconist's	**tabacaria**	tabakuh-**ree**-uh
toy shop	**loja de brinquedos**	**lozh**uh duh breeñ**kay**-doosh

Food (general)

beef	**a carne de vaca**	karn duh **vah**-kuh
biscuits	**as bolachas**	boo**lah**-shush
bread	**o pão**	powñ
bread (brown)	**o pão integral**	powñ eeñtuh-**grahl**

bread roll	**o papo-seco/ carcaça**	**pah**-poo-**seh**-koo/kar**ka**sa
butter	**a manteiga**	muñ**tay**-guh
cakes	**os bolos**	**boh**-loosh
cheese	**o queijo**	**kay**-zhoo
chicken	**o frango**	**fruñ**goo
coffee	**o café**	kuh-**fe**
cream	**a nata**	**nah**-tuh
crisps	**as batatas fritas**	bu**tah**-tush **free**tush
eggs	**os ovos**	**oh**-voosh
fish	**o peixe**	paysh
flour	**a farinha**	fa**reen**-yuh
ham (cooked)	**o fiambre**	fee-**uñ**-bruh
ham (cured)	**o presunto**	pruh-**zoon**too
honey	**o mel**	mel
jam	**a compota**	koñ**pot**uh
lamb	**o borrego**	bo**ray**-goo
margarine	**a margarina**	marguh-**ree**nuh
marmalade	**o doce de laranja**	dohss duh la**ruñ**zhuh
milk	**o leite**	layt
olive oil	**o azeite**	a**zayt**
orange juice	**o sumo de laranja**	**soo**moo duh la**ruñ**zhuh
pasta	**as massas**	**mass**ush

pepper	**a pimenta**	pee**meñ**tuh
pork	**a carne de porco**	karn duh **por**koo
rice	**o arroz**	a**rrosh**
salt	**o sal**	sal
(vegetable) stock cube	**o caldo de legumes**	**kahl**doo duh le**goo**mush
(meat) stock cube	**o caldo de carne**	**kahl**doo duh karn
sugar	**o açúcar**	uh-**soo**kar
tea	**o chá**	shah
vinegar	**o vinagre**	vee**nah**-gruh

Food (fruit and veg)

Fruit

apples	**as maçãs**	muh-**suñsh**
apricots	**os damascos**	muh-**mash**koosh
bananas	**as bananas**	buh-**nah**-nush
cherries	**as cerejas**	suh-**ray**-zhush
grapefruit	**a toranja**	too**ruñ**zhuh
grapes	**as uvas**	**oo**vush
lemon	**o limão**	lee**mowñ**
melon	**o melão**	me**lowñ**

nectarines	as nectarinas	nek-tuh-**ree**nush
oranges	as laranjas	la**ruñ**zhush
peaches	os pêssegos	**pay**-suh-goosh
pears	as peras	**pay**-rush
pineapple	o ananás	anuh-**nash**
plums	as ameixas	a**may**-shush
raspberries	as framboesas	frum-**bway**-zush
strawberries	os morangos	moo**ruñ**goosh
watermelon	a melancia	meluñ-**see**-uh

Vegetables

asparagus	os espargos	**shpar**goosh
aubergine	a beringela	bereeñ-**zhe**luh
cabbage	a couve	kohv
carrots	as cenouras	suh-**noh**-rush
cauliflower	a couve-flor	kohv-**flor**
courgettes	as courgettes	koor**zhetsh**
french beans	o feijão verde	fay-**zhowñ** vehrd
garlic	o alho	**ahl**-yoo
leek	o alho-francês	**ahl**-yoo frañ-**sesh**
lettuce	a alface	al**fass**
mushrooms	os cogumelos	koogoo-**mel**oosh
onions	as cebolas	suh-**bol**ush
peas	as ervilhas	ehr**veel**-yush
peppers	os pimentos	pee**meñ**toosh

potatoes	**as batatas**	bu**tah**-tush
spinach	**os espinafres**	shpee**naf**rush
tomato	**o tomate**	too-**mat**
turnips	**os nabos**	**nah**-boosh

Clothes

Size for clothes is **a medida** – shoes is **o número**.

May I try this on?	**Posso provar isto?** **poss**oo proo**var eesh**too?
Where are the changing rooms?	**Onde é o gabinete de provas?** **oñ**duh e oo gabee**net** duh **prov**ush?
Have you a size...?	**Tem uma medida...?** tayñ **oo**muh muh**dee**-duh...?
bigger/smaller	**maior/mais pequena** may**or**/mysh puh-**kay**nuh
It's too...	**É muito...** e **mweeñ**too...
short/long	**curto/comprido** **koor**too/koñ**pree**doo
I'm just looking	**Só estou a ver** so shtoh uh vehr
I'll take it	**Quero comprar** **kehr**oo koñ**prar**

Shopping

women's sizes		men's suit sizes		shoe sizes			
UK	EU	UK	EU	UK	EU	UK	EU
8	36	36	46	2	35	7	40
10	38	38	48	3	36	8	41
12	40	40	50	4	37	9	42
14	42	42	52	5	38	10	43
16	44	44	54	6	39	11	44
18	46	46	56				

YOU MAY HEAR...

De que medida? duh kuh muh**dee**-duh?	What size?
Quer provar? kehr proo**var**?	Do you want to try it on?
Que número veste/ calça? kuh **noo**meroo **vee**shtuh/ **kah**lsuh?	What size/shoe size are you?

Clothes (articles)

belt	**o cinto**	**seeñ**too
blouse	**a blusa**	**bloo**zuh
bra	**o soutien**	soot-**yañ**

coat	**o casaco**	ka**zah**-koo
dress	**o vestido**	vesh**tee**doo
hat	**o chapéu**	sha**pay**-oo
hat (woollen)	**a boina**	**boy**nuh
jacket	**o blusão**	bloo**zowñ**
knickers	**as cuecas**	**kwe**kush
nightdress	**a camisa de dormir**	kuh-**mee**zuh duh door**meer**
pyjamas	**o pijama**	pee**zhah**-muh
sandals	**as sandálias**	suñ**dahl**-yush
scarf (wool)	**o cachecol**	kashu-**kol**
shirt	**a camisa**	kuh-**mee**zuh
shorts	**os calções**	kal**soyñsh**
skirt	**a saia**	**sy**-uh
slippers	**as chinelas**	shee**nel**ush
socks	**as peúgas**	**pew**-gush
suit	**o fato**	**fah**-too
swimsuit	**o fato de banho**	**fah**-too duh **bun**-yoo
tie	**a gravata**	gruh-**vah**-tuh
tights	**os collants**	ko**lañsh**
tracksuit	**o fato de treino**	**fah**-too duh **tray**-noo
trousers	**as calças**	**kahl**sush
t-shirt	**a camisola**	kuhmee**zoh**-luh
underpants	**as cuecas**	**kwe**kush

Maps and guides

Have you...?	**Tem...?** tayñ...?
a map of (name town)	**um mapa de...** ooñ **mah**-puh duh...
of the region	**da região** duh ruzh-**yowñ**
a guide book	**algum guia** al**gooñ ghee**-uh
a leaflet	**algum folheto** al**gooñ** fool-**yet**oo
in English	**em inglês** ayñ eeñ**glaysh**
Can you show me where ... is on the map?	**Pode-me mostrar onde fica ... no mapa?** **pod**-muh moosh-**trar oñ**duh **fee**kuh ... noo **mah**-puh?

Post office

Most post offices are open from 9 a.m. to 6 p.m. Monday to Friday, but this varies from town to town. A few are open until 1 p.m. on Saturdays. Check times in small towns.

os correios oosh koo**rray**oosh	post office
o marco do correio oo **mar**koo doo koo**rray**oo	postbox
os selos oosh **sel**oosh	stamps

Is there a post office near here?	**Há algum correio aqui perto?** a al**gooñ** koo**rray**oo uh-**kee** **pehr**too?
I'd like stamps for ... postcards to Great Britain	**Queria selos para ... postais para a Grã-Bretanha** **kree**-uh **sel**oosh **pa**ruh ... poosh-**tysh** prah grañ-bruh-**tun**-yuh
How much is it to send this parcel?	**Quanto custa mandar este embrulho?** **kwuñ**too **koosh**tuh muñ**dar** aysht aym-**brool**-yoo?
first class	**por correio azul** poor koo**rray**oo a**zool**

Technology

o cartão de memória kar**towñ duh** meh-**mor**-yuh	memory card
imprimir eempreem**eer**	to print

a máquina fotográfica digital **mak**eenuh foto**grah**-feekuh deezhee**tahl**	digital camera
o cigarro eletrónico see-**gah**-rroo eeleh**tron**eekoo	e-cigarette

Can you repair...?	**Pode reparar...?** pode ruh-pa**rar**...?
my screen	**o meu ecrã** oo mayoo eh**krañ**
my keypad	**o meu teclado** oo mayoo tehk**lah**doo
my lens	**a minha lente** uh **meen**-ya lent
my charger	**o meu carregador** oo **may**oo kahrrehgah**dor**
I want to print my photos	**Quero imprimir as minhas fotos** **kay**roo eempreem**eer** uhs **meen**yush fohtoosh
I have it on my USB	**Está na minha pen** shtuh nuh **meen**yah pen
I have it on my e-mail	**Está no meu email** shtuh noo **may**oo email

Leisure

Sightseeing and tourist office

The tourist office is called **Turismo**. If you are looking for somewhere to stay, they should have details of hotels, campsites, etc.

Where is the tourist office?	**Onde é o turismo?** **oñ**duh e oo too**reezh**-moo?
We'd like to go to...	**Gostariamos de ir a...** gooshtuh-**ree**-uhmoosh duh eer uh...
Is it OK to take children?	**É permitido levar crianças?** e permee**tee**-doo luh-**var** kree-**uñ**sush?
Are there any excursions?	**Há algumas excursões?** a al**goo**mush shkoor-**soyñsh**?
How much does it cost to get in?	**Quanto custa a entrada?** **kwuñ**too **koosh**tuh uh ayn**trah**-duh?
Are there any reductions for...?	**Fazem descontos para...?** fa**zayñ** dush**koñ**toosh **pa**ruh...?
children	**crianças** kree-**uñ**sush

Leisure

students	**estudantes** shtoo**duñtsh**
unemployed people	**desempregados** duh-zaympruh-**gah**-doosh
senior citizens	**terceira idade** ter**say**ruh ee**dahd**
Can I visit ... with a wheelchair?	**Posso visitar ... com cadeira de rodas?** **poss**oo veezee**tar** ... koñ kuh-**day**-ruh duh **rod**ush?

Leisure

Entertainment

There are traditional festivities in June dedicated to the **Santos Populares**. Saints vary in popularity depending on the location; **Santo António** (St Anthony) is very popular in Lisbon, and **São João** (St John) in Porto. A beautiful street parade takes place all over Lisbon, the festivities being seen as a competition between Lisbon's **bairros** (neighbourhoods). You'll find dancing, eating and drinking in the streets of various regions of the city (**Bairro Alto**, **Alfama** and **Mouraria** to name a few).

What is there to do in the evenings?	**Que se pode fazer à noite?** kuh suh pod fa**zehr** a noyt?

Nightlife

Where can I go clubbing?	**Onde é que há discotecas?** **oñ**duh eh kuh a deeshkoh**teh**kash?

bar	**o bar** bar
gay bar/club	**o clube gay** kloob gay
gig	**o concerto** koñ**sehr**-too
music festival	**o festival de música** fushtee**vahl** duh **moo**zeekuh
nightclub	**o clube noturno** kloob noh**toor**noo
party	**a party** p**ar**tee
pub	**o pub** pub

Out and about

Where can I/ we go...?	**Onde se pode...?** **oñ**duh suh pod...?
fishing	**pescar** push**kar**
walking	**andar** uñ**dar**

Are there any good beaches near here?	**Há algumas praias boas aqui perto?** a al**goo**mush **pry**-ush **boh**-ush uh-**kee pehr**too?
Is there a swimming pool?	**Há piscina?** a peesh-**see**nuh?

YOU MAY HEAR...	
Proibido nadar proee-**bee**doo nuh-**dar**	No swimming
Proibido mergulhar proee-**bee**doo mehrgool**yar**	No diving

What's on at the cinema?	**Qual é o programa no cinema?** kwal e oo proo**gruh**-muh noo see**nay**-muh?
What's on at the theatre?	**Qual é o programa de teatro?** kwal e oo proo**gruh**-muh duh tee-**ah**-troo?
I'd like two tickets...	**Queria dois bilhetes...** **kree**-uh doysh beel-**yetsh**...
for tonight	**para esta noite** **pa**ruh **esh**tuh noyt
for tomorrow night	**para amanhã à noite** **pa**ruh amun-**yañ** a noyt

adventure centre	**o centro de aventuras**	sehñtroo duh ahveñ**too**rush
art gallery	**a galeria de arte**	galeh-**ree**-uh duh art

boat hire	**o aluguer de barcos**	aloo**gehr** duh **bar**koosh
camping	**o campismo**	kuñ**peesh**-moo
museum	**o museu**	moo-**zay**-oo
piercing	**o piercing**	piercing
tattoo	**a tatuagem**	tatoo-**ah**zhayñ
theme park	**o parque temático**	park teh**mah**teekoo
water park	**o parque aquático**	park ak**wah**teekoo
zoo	**o jardim zoológico**	zhar**deeñ** zoo-oh**lozh**eekoo

Music

Are there any good concerts on?	**Há algum bom concerto por aqui?** a al**goom** boñ koñ**sehr**-too poor uh-**kee**?
Where can we hear some fado/folk music?	**Onde podemos ouvir o fado/folclore?** **oñ**duh poo**deh**-moosh oh-**veer** oo **fah**-doo/folk**lo**ruh?

folk	**folk**	fohlk
hip-hop	**hip-hop**	eep-op

pop	**pop**	pop
reggae	**reggae**	reh**ge**
rock	**rock**	rok
techno	**techno**	**tehk**noo

Sport

o campo	oo **kum**poo	pitch/court
empatar	eñpuh**tar**	to draw a match
ganhar	gun-**yar**	to win

Where can I/we...?	**Onde se pode...?** **oñ**duh suh pod...?
play tennis	**jogar ténis** zhoo**gar ten**eesh
play golf	**jogar golfe** zhoo**gar** golf
go swimming	**nadar** nuh-**dar**
see some football	**ver futebol** vehr foot**bol**
How much is it per hour?	**Quanto é por hora?** **kwuñ**too e poor **or**uh?
I want to try...	**Gostava de experimentar...** goosh**tah**vuh duh eysh**pehr**eementar...

I've never done this before	**Nunca fiz isto** **noon**kuh feezh **eesh**too
Do they hire out...?	**Alugam...?** aloo**gowñ**...?
rackets	**raquetes** ra**ket**ush
golf clubs	**tacos de golfe** **tah**-koosh duh golf
Where's the best place to go fishing?	**Qual é o melhor lugar para ir pescar?** kwal e oo mel-**yor** loo**gar** paruh eer pesh**kar**?
Do you have a guide to local walks?	**Tem algum guia de caminhadas locais?** tayñ al**gooñ ghee**-uh duh kameen-**yah**dush loo**kysh**?
How many kilometres is the walk?	**De quantos quilómetros é o passeio?** duh **kwuñ**toosh kee**lom**etroosh e oo pa**ssay**oo?

cycling	**ciclismo**	see**klee**zhmoo
dancing	**ir dançar**	eer dahn**sar**
kayaking	**fazer caiaque**	fah**zehr** ka**yak**
rock climbing	**o alpinismo**	alpee**neezh**moo
snowboarding	**fazer snowboard**	fah**zehr** snowboard
volleyball	**o voleibol**	**voll**eyball
water-skiing	**o esqui aquático**	ski ak**wah**teekoo
windsurfing	**o windsurf**	**wind**surf

Leisure

Communications

Telephone and mobile

The international code for Portugal is **00 351** plus the Portuguese number. For calls within Portugal, landline numbers have nine digits and there are no area codes.

atender	uhteñ**der**	to pick up
desligar	dushlee**gar**	to hang up

I want to make a phone call	**Quero fazer uma chamada** **keh**roo fa**zehr oo**muh shuh-**mah**-duh
What is the number of your mobile?	**Qual é o número do seu telemóvel?** kwal e oo **noo**meroo doo **say**oo tuh-luh-**mo**vel?
My mobile number is...	**O meu número de telemóvel é...** oo mayoo **noo**meroo duh tuh-luh-**mo**vel e...
I would like to speak to...	**Queria falar com...** **kree**-uh fa**lar** koñ...

Senhor Lopes, please	**O Sr. Lopes, por favor** oo sun-**yor** lopsh, poor fuh-**vor**
I will call back later	**Volto a ligar mais tarde** **vol**too uh lee**gar** mysh tard
I can't get through	**Não consigo ligar** nowñ koñ**see**goo lee**gar**
Do you have a ... charger/cable?	**Tem um carregador/cabo para...?** tayñ kahrrehgah**dor/kah**boo **pa**ruh...?
Can I borrow your...?	**Empresta-me o seu/a sua...?** aym**presh**-tuh-muh oo **say**oo/ uh**soo**-uh...?
smartphone	**o smartphone** **smart**-fohn
I have an e-ticket on my phone	**Tenho um bilhete eletrónico no meu telemóvel** **ten**-yoo ooñ beel**yet** eele**troh**neekoo noo **may**oo tuh-luh-**mo**vel
I need to phone a UK/a US/ an Australian number	**Preciso de ligar para a Inglaterra/a América/ a Austrália** pre-**see**zoo leegar **pa**ruh uh eeñ-gluh-**terr**-uh/ uh uh**meh**reekuh/ uh ow**strah**leeya

FACE TO FACE
Estou/Alô/Sim? shtoh/a**loh**/seeñ? Hello?
Posso falar com...? **poss**oo fa**lar** koñ...? Can I speak to...?
Quem fala? kayñ **fah**-luh? Who is speaking?
Daqui é o Jim Brown duh-**kee** e oo jim brown This is Jim Brown
Um momento ooñ mo**meñ**-too Just a moment

YOU MAY HEAR...	
Não desligue nowñ duzh-**leeg**	Hold on
Está impedido shta eeñpuh-**dee**doo	It's engaged
Pode ligar mais tarde? pod lee**gar** mysh tard?	Can you try again later?
Quer deixar um recado? kehr day**shar** ooñ re**kah**-doo?	Do you want to leave a message?

É favor desligar o telemóvel e fuh-**vor** dushlee**gar** oo tuh-luh-**mo**vel	Please turn off mobiles

Text messaging

Although there are some abbreviated expressions in Portuguese used for texting and social media, note that Portuguese people regularly use the most popular text messaging terms in English too.

bjs	**beijos**	kisses
obgd	**obrigado(a)**	thanks
tb	**também**	also
pq	**porque**	because
qd	**quando**	when
+ trd	**mais tarde**	later
1 mnt	**1 minuto**	one minute

text (message) **SMS**
ess em ess

to send a text (message) **mandar um SMS**
muñ**dar** ooñ ess em ess

E-mail

The Portuguese for e-mail is **correio eletrónico** (koo**rray**oo ele**troh**-neekoo) although most people use the word **email**.

What is your e-mail address?	**Qual é o seu endereço de email?** kwal e oo **say**oo eñ-duh-**re**soo duh e-**mayl**?
How do you spell it?	**Como se soletra?** **koh**-moo suh soo**let**ruh?
My e-mail address is...	**O meu email é...** oo **may**oo e-**mayl** e...
clare.smith@collins.co.uk	**clare.smith@collins.co.uk** clare **poon**too smith arr**oh**-buh collins **poon**too co **poon**too oo-ka-puh

Internet

página principal **pah**-zheenuh preensee**pahl**	home
nome de usuário nom doo ooz**war**yoo	username
navegar nave**gar**	to browse
motor de busca moo**tor** duh **boosh**kuh	search engine

senha **sen**-yuh	password
contacte-nos koñ**takt**-noosh	contact us
voltar ao menu vol**tar** ow me**noo**	back to menu
wi-fi wi-fi	Wi-Fi
a rede social red soosee-**al**	social network
o aplicativo apleeka**tee**voo	app
o portátil poor**tah**teel	laptop
o tablet **ta**blet	tablet

What is the Wi-Fi password? **Qual é a senha da internet?** kwal eh uh **sen**-yuh duh **in**ternet?

Do you have free Wi-Fi? **Tem internet grátis?** tayñ **in**ternet **grah**teesh?

Add me on Facebook **Adicione-me no Facebook** uh**dees**eeon-muh noo **Face**book

Is there a 3G/4G signal? **Há sinal 3G/4G?** a see**nahl** 3G/4G?

I need to access my webmail **Preciso de aceder ao meu mail** pre-**see**zoo duh asuh**dehr** aow **may**oo mail

I would like to use Skype **Gostava de usar o Skype** goosh**tah**vuh duh ooz**ar** oo Skype

Communications

Practicalities

Money

Banks are generally open from 8.30 a.m. to 3 p.m. Monday to Friday.

dólares **doh**laruhsh	dollars
libras leebrush	pounds
a taxa de câmbio tasha duh **kuñ**byoo	exchange rate

Where is the bank?	**Onde é o banco?** **oñ**duh e oo **buñ**koo?
Where can I/ we change some money?	**Onde se pode trocar dinheiro?** **oñ**duh suh pod troo**kar** deen-**yay**-roo?
What is the exchange rate for...?	**Qual é a taxa de câmbio de...?** kwahl e uh **tash**a duh **kuñ**byoo doo...?
When does the bank open/ close?	**Quando abre/fecha o banco?** **kwuñ**doo **ah**-bruh/**fay**shuh oo **buñ**koo?

Can I pay with pounds/euros? **Posso pagar em libras/euros?** **poss**oo puh-**gar** ayñ **lee**brush/ **eoo**-rosh?

Paying

a conta uh **koñ**tuh	bill
a caixa uh **ky**-shuh	cash desk
a fatura uh fa**too**ruh	invoice
pague na caixa **pah**-guh nuh **ky**-shuh	pay at the cash desk
o recibo oo ruh-**see**boo	receipt
só dinheiro soh deen-**yay**-roo	cash only
levantar dinheiro leh-vuñ**tar** deen-**yay**-roo	to withdraw money
o cartão Multibanco kar**towñ** mooltee-**buñ**koo	debit card
o cartão de crédito kar**towñ** **duh** **kred**eetoo	credit card
o pagamento sem contacto paguh**meñ**too sayñ koñ**tak**too	contactless payment

o cartão de viagem pré-pago kar**towñ** duh vee**ah**jayñ pre-puh-**go**	prepaid currency card

How much is it?	**Quanto é?** **kwuñ**too e?
Can I pay...?	**Posso pagar...?** **poss**oo puh-**gar**...?
by credit card	**com cartão de crédito** koñ kar**towñ** duh **kred**eetoo
by cheque	**por cheque** poor shek
Is service included?	**O serviço está incluído?** oo ser**vee**soo shta eeñ-**klwee**doo?
Is VAT included?	**O IVA está incluído?** oo ee**vuh** shta eeñ-**klwee**doo?
Please can I have a receipt?	**Pode-me dar um recibo por favor?** **pod**-muh dar ooñ ruh-**see**boo poor fuh-**vor**?
Do I pay in advance?	**Paga-se adiantado?** **pah**-guh-suh adyuñ-**tah**-doo?
Where do I pay?	**Onde se paga?** **oñ**duh suh **pah**-guh?
Can I pay in cash?	**Posso pagar em dinheiro?** possoo puh-**gar** ayñ deen-**yay**-roo?

Where is the nearest cash machine?	**Onde fica o Multibanco mais próximo?** **oñ**duh **fee**kuh oo mooltee-**buñ**koo mysh **pross**eemoo?
Is there a credit card charge?	**Há uma taxa de utilização do cartão de crédito?** a oomuh tasha duh ooteeleeza**sowñ** doo kar**towñ duh kred**eetoo?
Is there a discount for senior citizens/ for children?	**Há desconto para a terceira idade/para crianças?** a dushkontoo **pa**ruh a ter**say**ruh ee**dahd**/**pa**ruh kree-**uñ**sush?
Can you write down the price?	**Pode escrever o preço?** pod eesh-kreh-**vehr oo pray**-soo?

Practicalities

Luggage

a conta uh **koñ**tuh	bill
a recolha de bagagem uh re**kol**-yuh duh buh-**gah**-zhayñ	baggage reclaim
o carrinho oo ka**rreen**-yoo	trolley

My luggage hasn't arrived	**A minha bagagem não chegou** uh **meen**-yuh buh-**gah**-zhayñ nowñ shuh-**goh**
My suitcase has arrived damaged	**A minha mala chegou danificada** uh **meen**-yuh **mah**-luh shuh-**goh** duhneefee-**kah**-duh

Complaints

This is out of order	**Isto não funciona** **eesh**too nowñ foonss-**yo**nuh
light/heating	**a luz/o aquecimento** uh loosh/oo akuh-see**meñ**too
air conditioning	**o ar condicionado** oo ar koñdeess-yoo**nah**-doo
It's dirty	**Está sujo** shta **soo**zhoo
It's faulty	**Tem um defeito** tayñ ooñ duh-**fay**-too
I want a refund	**Quero um reembolso** **kehr**oo ooñ ree-aym-**bol**soo

Practicalities

Problems

Can you help me?	**Pode-me ajudar?** **pod**-muh azhoo**dar**?
I only speak a little Portuguese	**Só falo um pouco de português** so **fah**-loo ooñ **poh**koo duh poortoo-**gaysh**
Does anyone here speak English?	**Há aqui alguém que fale inglês?** a uh-**kee** al**gayñ** kuh **fah**-luh eeñ**glaysh**?
What's the matter?	**Que se passa?** kuh suh **pass**uh?
I would like to speak to whoever is in charge	**Queria falar com o encarregado** **kree**-uh fa**lar** koñ oo aynkuh-rray-**gah**-doo
I'm lost	**Estou perdido(a)** shtoh per**dee**doo(uh)
How do I get to...?	**Como se vai a...?** **koh**-moo suh vy uh...?
I've missed...	**Perdi...** per**dee**...
my train	**o meu comboio** oo **may**oo koñ**boy**oo
my connection	**a minha ligação** uh **meen**-yuh leeguh-**sowñ**

Practicalities

The coach has left without me	**O autocarro partiu sem mim** oo owtoo-**karr**oo part**yoo** sayñ meeñ
Can you show me how this works?	**Pode-me mostrar como funciona isto?** **pod**-muh moosh**trar koh**-moo foonss-**yo**nuh **eesh**too?
I have lost my purse	**Perdi o meu porta-moedas** per**dee** oo **may**oo portuh-**mway**-dush
I need to get to...	**Preciso de ir a...** pre-**see**zoo deer uh...
Leave me alone!	**Deixe-me em paz!** **day**-shu-muh ayñ pash!
Go away!	**Vá-se embora!** **vah**-suh aym**boh**-ruh!
Where can I recycle this?	**Onde posso reciclar isto?** **oñ**duh possoo ruhsee**klahr** **eesh**too?
I need to access my online banking	**Preciso de aceder à minha conta bancária online** pre-**see**zoo duh asuh**dehr** aow meenyuh **koñ**tuh ban**kah**reeya online
Do you have wheelchairs?	**Tem cadeiras de rodas?** tayñ kuh-**day**-rush duh **rod**ush?
elderly	**idosos** ee**doh**zoosh

Emergencies

The number for the emergency services is **112** (ambulance, fire and rescue, police). Calls are answered in English as well as in Portuguese.

a polícia uh poo**leess**-yuh	police
a ambulância uh uñboo**luñss**-yuh	ambulance
os bombeiros oos boñ**bay**-roosh	fire brigade
as urgências as oor-**zhayñ**see-ush	A&E

Help!	**Socorro!** soo**korr**oo!
Fire!	**Fogo!** **foh**-goo!
Can you help me?	**Pode-me ajudar?** **pod**-muh azhoo**dar**?
There's been an accident!	**Houve um acidente!** ohv ooñ asee**deñt**!
Someone is injured	**Há um ferido** a ooñ fe**ree**doo

Practicalities

Call...	**Chame...** sham...
the police	**a polícia** uh poo**leess**-yuh
an ambulance	**uma ambulância** **oo**muh amboo**luñss**-yuh
Where's the police station?	**Onde é a esquadra?** **oñ**duh e uh **shkwah**-druh?
I want to report a theft	**Quero participar um roubo** **kehr**oo purteesee**par** ooñ **roh**-boo
I've been attacked	**Fui agredido(a)** fwee agruh-**dee**-doo(uh)
Someone's stolen my...	**Roubaram-me...** roh-**bah**-rowñ-muh...
bag	**a mala** uh **mah**-luh
passport	**o passaporte** oo passuh-**port**
money	**o dinheiro** oo deen-**yay**-roo
My car's been broken into	**Assaltaram-me o carro** assal-**tah**-rowñ-muh oo **karr**oo
My car's been stolen	**Roubaram-me o carro** roh-**bah**-rowñ-muh oo **karr**oo
I've been raped	**Fui violada** fwee vyo**lah**duh
I am lost	**Estou perdido(a)** shtoh per**dee**doo(uh)

I want to speak to a policewoman	**Quero falar com uma mulher-polícia** **kehr**oo fa**lar** koñ **oo**muh mool-**yehr** poo**leess**-yuh
I need to make an urgent telephone call	**Preciso de fazer uma chamada urgente** pre-**see**zoo duh fa**zehr** **oo**muh shuh-**mah**-duh oor**zheñt**
I need a report for my insurance	**Preciso de um relatório para o meu seguro** pre-**see**zoo dooñ rela**tor**yoo pro **may**oo se**goo**roo
I didn't know the speed limit	**Não sabia qual era o limite de velocidade** nowñ suh-**bee**-uh kwal **e**ruh oo lee**meet** duh vuh-loossee-**dahd**
How much is the fine?	**Quanto é a multa?** **kwuñ**too e uh **mool**tuh?

YOU MAY HEAR...

Posso ajudar? **poss**oo uzhoo**dar**?	Can I help you?
Passou a luz vermelha pa**ssoh** uh loosh ver**mel**-yuh	You went through a red light

Practicalities

Health

Pharmacy

a farmácia uh far**mass**-yuh	pharmacy
a farmácia de serviço uh far**mass**-yuh duh ser**vee**ssoo	duty chemist
a receita médica uh re**say**tuh **med**eekuh	prescription

Have you something for...?	**Tem alguma coisa para...?** tayñ al**goo**muh **koy**-zuh **pa**ruh...?
a headache	**a dor de cabeça** uh dor duh kuh-**beh**-suh
car sickness	**o enjoo** oo eñ**zhoh**-oo
diarrhoea	**a diarreia** uh dee-uh-**rray**uh
I have a rash	**Tenho uma irritação de pele** **ten**-yoo **oo**muh ee-rreetuh-**sowñ** duh pel

Health

Is it safe for children?	**Pode-se dar às crianças?** **pod**-suh dar ash kree-**uñ**sush?
How much should I give?	**Quanto devo dar?** **kwuñ**too **deh**-voo dar?

asthma	**a asma**	**azh**muh
condom	**o preservativo**	pruzehrvuh**tee**voo
contact lenses	**as lentes de contacto**	leñtsh duh koñ**tak**too
inhaler	**o inalador**	eenahlah**dor**
morning-after pill	**a pílula do dia seguinte**	uh **pee**looluh doo deeya seh**giñt**
mosquito bite	**a picada de mosquito**	pee**kah**duh duh moosh**kee**too
mosquito repellent	**o repelente de mosquitos**	ruhpuh**lent** duh moos**kee**toosh
painkillers	**os analgésicos**	anal**zheh**-zeekoosh
period	**o período**	puhree**yoo**doo
the Pill	**a pílula**	uh **pee**looluh
tampon	**o tampão**	tañ**powñ**

Health

YOU MAY HEAR...	
Três vezes por dia antes/com/depois das refeições traysh **veh**-zush poor **dee**-uh uñtsh/koñ/duh**poysh** dush ruh-fay-**soyñsh**	Three times a day before/with/after meals

Doctor

In Portuguese the possessive (my, his, her, etc.) is generally not used with parts of the body, e.g.

My head hurts **Dói-me a cabeça**

My hands are dirty **Tenho as mãos sujas**

o hospital oo oshpee**tahl**	hospital
o banco (hospital) oo **buñ**koo oshpee**tahl**	casualty department
as horas de consulta ush **o**rush duh koñ**sool**tuh	surgery hours

FACE TO FACE
Não me sinto bem nowñ muh **seeñ**too bayñ I don't feel well

Health

Tem febre?
tayñ **feb**ruh?
Do you have a temperature?

Não, mas dói-me aqui
nowñ, mash **doy**-muh uh-**kee**
No, but I have a pain here

I need a doctor	**Preciso de um médico** pre-**see**zoo dooñ **med**eekoo
My son/ daughter is ill	**O meu filho/A minha filha está doente** oo **may**oo **feel**-yoo/uh **meen**-yuh **feel**-yuh shta doo-**eñt**
(S)he has a temperature	**Ele(a) tem febre** ayl(uh) tayñ **feb**ruh
I'm diabetic	**Sou diabético(a)** soh dee-uh-**bet**eekoo(uh)
I'm pregnant	**Estou grávida** shtoh **grah**-veeduh
I'm allergic to penicillin	**Sou alérgico(a) a penicilina** soh a**lehr**-zheekoo(uh) uh punee-see**lee**nuh
I'm allergic to ...	**Sou alérgico(a) a ...** soh a**lehr**-zheekoo(uh) a ...
pollen	**pólen** **poh**leñ
dairy	**laticínios** lahtee**seen**eeyoos
gluten	**glúten** **gloo**teñ
nuts	**frutos secos** **froo**toos **seh**koosh

Health

I have a prescription for...	**Tenho uma receita para...** **ten**-yoo ooma re**say**tuh paruh...
I've run out of medication	**Acabaram-se-me os remédios** akuh-**bar**owñ-suh-muh oozh re**med**eeyoosh
I'm on the pill	**Tomo a pílula** **tom**oo uh **peel**oo-luh
My blood group is...	**O meu grupo sanguíneo é...** oo **may**oo **groo**poo suñ**geen**-yoo e...
Will I have to pay?	**Tenho que pagar?** **ten**-yoo kuh puh-**gar**?
I need a receipt for the insurance	**Preciso de um recibo para o seguro** pre-**see**zoo dooñ ruh-**see**boo pro se**goo**roo
A&E (accident and emergency)	**o serviço de urgências** ser**vee**soo duh oor**zheñ**seeyas
drug abuse	**a toxicodependência** toxeekohdeepen**deñ**seeya
epilepsy	**a epilepsia** epeeleh**psee**ya
food poisoning	**a intoxicação alimentar** eeñtokseekuh**sowñ** aleemeñ**tar**
GP (general practitioner)	**o/a médico(a) de clínica geral** **med**eekoo(uh) duh **klee**neekuh zheh**ral**
sprain	**o entorse** ayñ**torss**

STI/STD (sexually transmitted infection/ disease)	**a IST/a DST (a infeção/ a doença sexualmente transmissível)** IST/DST (a iñfeh**sowñ**/ a doo**ehñ**suh sexooal**meñ**tuh trañsmee**see**vel)	

YOU MAY HEAR...	
Tem de ser internado(a) tayñ duh sehr eentuhr**nah**doo(uh)	You will have to be admitted to hospital
Não é grave nowñ e grahv	It's not serious
Não ingerir álcool nowñ eenzhe**reer ahl**kol	Do not drink alcohol
Bebe? beb?	Do you drink?
Fuma? **foo**muh?	Do you smoke?
Consome drogas? consom **droh**guhsh?	Do you take drugs?

arm	**o braço**	**brah**ssoo
back	**as costas**	**kosh**tuhs
chest	**o peito**	**pay**too
ear	**a orelha**	oo-**rel**-yuh
ear (if the pain is inside)	**o ouvido**	oh**vee**doo
eye	**o olho**	**ohl**yoo
foot	**o pé**	peh

Health

head	**a cabeça**	kuh-**beh**-suh
heart	**o coração**	koora**sowñ**
leg	**a perna**	**payr**nuh
neck	**o pescoço**	puh**sko**ssoo
toe	**o dedo do pé**	**deh**doo doo peh
tooth	**o dente**	deñt
wrist	**o pulso**	**pool**soo

Dentist

o chumbo oo **shoom**boo	filling
a coroa uh koo-**roh**-uh	crown
a dentadura postiça uh deñtuh-**doo**ruh poosh-**tee**suh	denture

I need a dentist	**Preciso de um dentista** pre-**see**zoo dooñ deñ**teesh**tuh
I have toothache	**Tenho uma dor de dentes** **ten**-yoo **oo**muh dor duh **deñtsh**
Can you do a temporary filling?	**Pode pôr um chumbo provisório?** pod por ooñ **shoom**boo provee-**zor**yoo?

Health

It hurts (me)	**Dói-me** **doy**-muh
Can you give me something for the pain?	**Pode-me dar alguma coisa para a dor?** **pod**-muh dar al**goo**muh **koy**-zuh pra dor?

YOU MAY HEAR...

É preciso arrancar e pre-**see**zoo arruñ**kar**	It has to come out
Vou-lhe dar uma injecção **vol**-yuh dar **oo**muh eeñzhe**sowñ**	I'm going to give you an injection

Health

Eating out

Eating places

For eating out, mealtimes vary a lot. Generally speaking, lunch is served between 12.30 and 2 p.m. Dinner starts at 7 or 7.30 p.m. and goes on until 9.30 or 10 p.m.

Bar Serves drinks, coffee and snacks. Generally open all day. Look out for **pastéis de bacalhau** (cod cakes), **rissóis de camarão** (prawn rissoles) and **um prego** (a steak roll).

A área de piquenique Picnic area.

Casa de chá Literally a tea house, an elegant pâtisserie which serves a variety of drinks. Look out for **bolos** (mouth-watering cakes), **torradas** (toast) and **sandes** (sandwiches made with white bread rolls and often **queijo** (cheese), **fiambre** (ham) or **presunto** (cured ham)).

Pastelaria Pâtisserie or cake shop. Popular for snacks, soups and light meals.

Restaurante At restaurants, lunch is usually between 12.30 and 2.30 p.m. Dinner starts at 7 or 7.30 p.m. and goes on until 9.30 or 10 p.m.

Marisqueira Serves seafood and drinks.

Churrasqueira Restaurant serving barbecued food, mainly chicken. Most are take-away places.

Cervejaria Beer house serving good lager and savouries. It generally offers a good menu, often specialising in seafood or steak.

Tasca A small local tavern. Once cheap eating places, they are becoming gentrified.

Casa de pasto Simple, old-fashioned, restaurant usually offering good value meals at lunchtime. Some have become gentrified; others are still modest, cheap places.

In a bar/café

If you want a small, strong black coffee ask for **um café** (also known as **uma bica**). A small, white coffee is **um garoto**. An ordinary white coffee is **um café com leite**. A large (mug-sized) coffee **uma meia de leite**, and is **um galão** is the same but served in a tall glass. Tea is normally served in a teapot, weak and without any milk. If you order water, the waiter may ask '**natural ou fresca?**', **natural** means at room temperature, and **fresca** is cold.

a coffee	**um café** ooñ kuh-**fe**
a milky coffee	**um galão** ooñ ga**lowñ**
a lager	**uma cerveja** **oo**muh ser**vay**-zhuh
a (strong) tea...	**um chá (forte)...** ooñ shah (fort)...
with milk/lemon	**com leite/limão** koñ layt/lee**mowñ**
for me	**para mim** **pa**ruh meeñ
for him/her	**para ele/ela** **pa**ruh ayl/**ay**luh
with ice, please	**com gelo, por favor** koñ **zhay**-loo, poor fuh-**vor**
a bottle of mineral water	**uma garrafa de água mineral** **oo**muh ga**rrah**-fuh **dahg**-wuh meenuh-**rahl**
sparkling/still	**com gás/sem gás** koñ gahs/sayñ gahs

Other drinks to try

um chocolate a chocolate drink, served hot **quente** or cold **frio**

um chá de limão boiling water poured over fresh lemon peel. A refreshing drink after a meal or at any time

um batido de fruta fruit milkshake, such as strawberry (**morango**)

Reading the menu

Restaurants will have the menu displayed next to the entrance. If you don't want a full meal, it is better to go to a snack bar, **Pastelaria** (cake shop), **Casa de chá** (tea house) or **Cervejaria** (beer house).

Pratos Combinados These are likely to consist of ham, egg, chips, fresh salad, perhaps, sausage and/ or cheese and bread.

Pratos do Dia Dishes of the day, these are generally more economical and readily served than the à la carte menu.

Ementa do Dia Set-price menu, with 3 courses (starter, meat or fish and dessert). May include wine and an espresso.

Ementa Turística Set-price menu, as above, offering traditional dishes. The set-price menus may only be available for lunch.

Ementa	Menu (à la carte)
Entradas	Starters
Acepipes	Appetisers
Sopas	Soups
Peixe e Marisco	Fish and shellfish
Pratos de Carne	Meat dishes

Ovos	Eggs
Acompanhamentos	Side dishes
Legumes	Vegetables
Saladas	Salads
Sobremesa	Desserts
Queijos	Cheeses
Caseiro(a)	Homemade
Especialidade regional	Local delicacy

In a restaurant

It is considered good manners to always eat with the appropriate knife and fork for meat or fish, however it is acceptable to eat chicken or pizza with your hands. It's common to say **Bom apetite** before you start your meal and it's polite to wipe your mouth before and after sipping wine or water. For tipping, there is no fixed amount: 10% is considered fair, but not mandatory.

I'd like to book a table for ... people	**Queria reservar uma mesa para ... pessoas** **kree**-uh ruh-zer**var oo**muh **may**-zuh **pa**ruh ... puh-**so**-ush

for tonight...	**para esta noite...** **pa**ruh **esh**tuh noyt...
at 8 p.m.	**às 8 horas** ash **oy**too **or**ush
The menu, please	**A ementa, por favor** uh ee**meñ**tuh, poor fuh-**vor**
What is the dish of the day?	**Qual é o prato do dia?** kwal e oo **prah**-too doo **dee**-uh?
Do you have a children's menu?	**Tem uma ementa para crianças?** tayñ **oo**muh ee**meñ**tuh paruh kree-**uñ**sush?
I'll have this	**Quero isto** **kehr**oo **eesh**too
Can you recommend a local dish?	**Pode recomendar uma especialidade local?** pod ruh-koomeñ**dar oo**muh shpuh-syalee-**dahd** loo**kahl**?
Excuse me!	**Faz favor!** fash fuh-**vor**!
Please bring...	**Traga...** **trah**-guh...
more bread/ butter	**mais pão/manteiga** mysh powñ/muñ**tay**-guh
more water	**mais água** mysh **ahg**-wuh
a high chair	**uma cadeira alta** **oo**muh kuh-**day**-ruh **ahl**tuh

Eating out

another bottle	**outra garrafa** **oh**-truh ga**rrah**-fuh
the bill	**a conta** a **koñ**tuh
Is service included?	**O serviço está incluído?** oo ser**vee**soo shta eeñ-**klwee**doo?
Is there a set menu?	**Há uma ementa fixa?** a **oo**ma e**meñ**tuh **feek**suh?
We would like a table for ... people please	**Queríamos uma mesa para ... pessoas, por favor** **kree**-uhmoosh **oo**ma **may**-zuh para ... puh-**so**-ush, poor fuh-**vor**
This isn't what I ordered	**Não foi isto que pedi** nowñ foy eestoo kuh puh-**dee**
The ... is too...	**O/a ... está demasiado...** oo/uh ... shtah demaz**yah**doo...

cold	**frio(a)**	**free**-oo(uh)
greasy	**gorduroso (a)**	gordoo**ros**oo(uh)
rare	**malpassado(a)**	mal-puh-**sah**-doo(uh)
salty	**salgado(a)**	sal**gah**doo(uh)
spicy	**picante**	peek**ant**
warm	**morno(a)**	**mor**noo(uh)
well done	**bem passado(a)**	bayñ puh-**sah**-doo(uh)

Dietary requirements

Are there any vegetarian restaurants here?	**Há algum restaurante vegetariano aqui?** a al**gooñ** rushtoh-**ruñt** veh-zhuh-tuh-**ryah**-noo uh-**kee**?
Do you have any vegetarian dishes?	**Tem algum prato vegetariano?** tayñ al**gooñ prah**-too veh-zhuh-tuh-**ryah**-noo?
What fish dishes do you have?	**Que pratos de peixe tem?** kuh **prah**-toosh duh paysh tayñ?
Is it made with vegetable stock?	**É feito com caldo vegetal?** e **fay**-too koñ **kahl**doo veh-zhuh-**tahl**?
I have a ... allergy	**Tenho uma alergia a...** ten-yoo ooma alehr-**zhee**-uh uh...
Is it ...-free ?	**É sem...?** e sayñ...?
I don't eat...	**Não como...** nowñ como...

coeliac	**celíaco(a)**	**seel**eeyakoo(uh)
dairy	**o(s) laticínio(s)**	lahtee**seen**eeyoo(sh)
gluten	**o glúten**	**gloo**ten
halal	**halal**	a**lahl**
nuts	**os frutos secos**	**froo**toosh **seh**koosh

organic	**orgânico(a)**	oor**gah**neekoo(uh)
vegan	**o/a vegan**	**veh**gan
wheat	**o trigo**	**tree**goo

Wines and spirits

The **vinho de casa** (house wine) is normally quite good and inexpensive.

The wine list, please	**A lista de vinhos, por favor** uh **leesh**tuh duh **veen**-yoosh, poor fuh-**vor**
Can you recommend a good wine?	**Pode recomendar um bom vinho?** pod ruh-koomeñ**dar** ooñ boñ **veen**-yoo?
A bottle.../ A carafe...	**Uma garrafa.../Um jarro...** **oo**muh ga**rrah**-fuh.../ ooñ **zharr**oo...
of the house wine	**de vinho da casa** duh **veen**-yoo duh **kah**-zuh
of red wine	**de vinho tinto** duh **veen**-yoo **teeñ**too
of white wine	**de vinho branco** duh **veen**-yoo **bruñ**koo
of rosé wine	**de vinho rosé** duh **veen**-yoo roh-**ze**

Eating out

of 'green' wine	**de vinho verde** duh **veen**-yoo vehrd
of dry wine	**de vinho seco** duh **veen**-yoo **seh**-koo
of sweet wine	**de vinho doce** duh **veen**-yoo dohss
of a local wine	**de vinho da região** duh **veen**-yoo duh ruzh-**yowñ**
What liqueurs do you have?	**Que licores tem?** kuh lee-**korsh** tayñ?
A glass of port	**Um cálice de Porto** ooñ **kah**-leesuh duh **por**too
A glass of Boal (madeira)	**Um cálice de Boal** ooñ **kah**-leesuh duh boo-**ahl**

Types of port Porto

Port wines offer a wide variety of styles, making them suitable for all occasions and also for serving with food. The main types are:

White (which can be sweet or dry, so check the label). Good on its own or as an aperitif. It should be chilled and can be made into a long drink with a little ice and a twist of lemon.

Ruby is a blend of young ports, ready to drink, spicy and fruity. Sweet and ruby in colour. No need to decant.

Tawny is a blend from various harvests. It has a rich amber colour, a long finish and complex aroma.

Look for labels indicating its age (10, 20, 30 years old). It is ready to drink and does not need decanting. This is the most popular style.

Vintage Port is a wine from an exceptional declared harvest. Matured in wood for two or three years, it is bottled and continues to mature, for at least 10 years, or much longer. It must be decanted. It is dark and rich, becoming softer and more complex as it ages. There are intermediate styles (LBV, for example). The label should help.

Types of madeira Madeira

Madeira wines, like ports, can be served as an aperitif, for dessert or on any other occasion. The four categories are:

Sercial quite dry and pale

Verdelho less dry and slightly darker than **Sercial**

Boal richer-coloured and sweeter

Malvasia dark, very perfumed, full-bodied and very sweet

Whatever their category, these wines are always very aromatic and complex. The drier styles should be served chilled.

Menu reader

acelga swiss chard
acepipes appetisers
acompanhamentos side dishes
açorda typical Portuguese dish with bread
açorda com peixe frito thick bread soup accompanying fried fish
açorda de alho bread soup with garlic and beaten egg (generally served with fried fish)
açorda de marisco thick bread soup with shellfish and a beaten egg, typical of the Lisbon area
adocicado slightly sweet
água mineral com gás sparkling mineral water
água mineral sem gás still mineral water
aguardente brandy
albardado in batter
almoço lunch
almôndegas meatballs
amarguinha bitter-almond liqueur
amêijoas à Bulhão Pato clams with garlic and coriander
amêijoas ao natural natural steamed clams with herbs and lemon butter
aniz aniseed liqueur
arjamolho kind of gazpacho soup

arroz branco plain rice
arroz de Cabidela strongly seasoned risotto with chicken or rabbit, made using the blood of the animals and very dark in colour
arroz de ervilhas pea rice
arroz de frango chicken with rice
arroz de lampreia lamprey with rice
arroz de manteiga rice with butter
arroz doce rice pudding
assado roasted, baked
assado no forno oven-roasted
assado no espeto spit roasted
atum assado braised tuna with onions and tomatoes
atum de cebolada tuna steak with onions and tomato sauce
atum salpresado salted tuna dish
azeda sorrel
azedo/a sour
bacalhau salt cod
bacalhau à Brás traditional dish with salt cod, onion and matchstick potatoes all bound with scrambled eggs
bacalhau à Gomes de Sá good salt cod dish with layers of potatoes, onions and boiled eggs, laced with olive oil and baked
bacalhau com natas salt cod in cream sauce au gratin
bacalhau com todos salt cod poached with potatoes and vegetables

bacalhau na brasa salt cod grilled on charcoal, served with olive oil
barriga de freira a sweet made with yolks and sugar, slightly caramelised
batata doce sweet potato
batatas a murro jacket potatoes soaked in olive oil
batatas cozidas boiled potatoes
batatas fritas chips
batido de fruta fruit milkshake
besugo sea bream
bica small strong black coffee, espresso
bifana hot meat, normally pork tenderloin in a roll
bife steak (with chips and perhaps a fried egg)
bife à café steak in cream sauce topped with a fried egg (with chips)
bifinhos de vitela veal fillet with Madeira sauce
bitoque small steak with fried egg and chips
bola layered bread and cured meat pie
bola de Berlim round cake made of sweet dough fried in oil with or without filling and with granulated sugar on top; similar to a doughnut
bolachas de água e sal water biscuits (crackers)
boleimas cakes with a bread dough base
bolinhos de bacalhau cod croquettes
bolo caseiro homemade cake
bolo de chocolate chocolate cake
bolo de mel honey cake
bolo podre dark cake made with honey, olive oil and spices

borracho young pigeon, squab
broa a crusty rustic maize bread
bucho pork haggis
cabrito kid
cabrito assado roast kid with a spiced marinade
cabrito montês roebuck
caça game
...à caçadora hunter-style (poultry or game marinated in wine and garlic)
cachucho small sea bream
(café) carioca small, weak black coffee
café com leite white coffee
café duplo large cup of black coffee
café frio iced coffee
café galão large white coffee served in a tall glass
café garoto small white coffee
caju cashew nut
caldeirada fish stew
caldeirada à fragateira seafood stew, as prepared by fishermen
caldeirada de enguias eel stew
caldo broth
caldo verde green broth, made with shredded kale and potatoes with **chouriço** and olive oil
caneca roughly a pint of beer
canja chicken broth, thickened with rice or small pasta and chicken pieces
capilé drink with iced coffee, lemon rind and sugar
caracóis snails (small, cooked in a tasty broth)
carapau horse mackerel

caril curry
carioca de limão lemon peel infusion
carne assada roast meat
carne de porco à alentejana highly seasoned pork dish with clams, typical of the Alentejo
carne estufada braised meat
carnes frias cold meats
carta dos vinhos wine list
casa de chá tea-house
casa de pasto restaurant serving cheap, homely meals. Some have now become gentrified and are no longer cheap. Always check the menu with the prices on display.
cataplana meat, fish or shellfish dish cooked in a tomato sauce in a **cataplana** pot
cerveja à pressão draught beer
cerveja em garrafa bottled beer
cerveja preta dark ale
cervejaria beer house, serving food
chá com leite tea with milk
chá com limão tea with lemon
chá forte strong tea
chá de ervas/tisana herb tea
chanfana rich goat stew
cherne species of grouper with dark skin
chila type of pumpkin made into jam
chispalhada pig's trotter stew
chispe com feijão trotters with beans, cured meats and vegetables
chocos com tinta cuttlefish in its own ink

choquinhos com tinta squid in its ink
chouriço spicy smoked sausage
churrasco barbecued/cooked on charcoal
churrasqueira restaurant specialising in **frango à piri-piri** (barbecued chicken with or without chilli) and other grilled meats
coelho rabbit
coentrada with fresh coriander
coentros fresh coriander
colorau sweet paprika
cominho cumin seed
compota jam or compote
congro conger eel
coração heart
costeletas de porco pork chops
couve-de-bruxelas brussels sprouts
couve-flor cauliflower
couve-lombarda savoy cabbage
couve-roxa red cabbage
cozido boiled or poached
cozido à Madeirense boiled Madeira-style pork and vegetables, with pumpkin and couscous
cravinhos cloves
croissants com fiambre ham-filled croissants
croissants recheados filled croissants
croquetes de carne meat croquettes
cru raw
cuba livre rum and Coke
digestivo digestive, e.g. brandy
dobrada tripe

doces de amêndoa marzipan sweets
doce de fruta jam
doce de laranja marmalade
eirós large eel
empadão de batata shepherd's pie
empadas small chicken or veal pies
enguias fritas fried eels
ensopado fish or meat stew served on bread slices
ensopado de borrego rich lamb stew served on bread slices
entradas starters
entrecosto spare ribs
ervilhas com paio e ovos peas with garlic sausage and poached eggs
escabeche a sauce containing vinegar, normally served over cold fried fish
escalfado poached
espada the name given in Madeira to **peixe espada** (scabbard fish)
esparregado usually spinach purée with garlic, but can be made with other green vegetables
espetada kebab
esplanada open-air restaurant/café
estufado braised
extra-seco extra-dry
farinheira sausage made with flour and pork fat
fartes de batata square cakes of sweet potato purée with spices and almonds
fataça grey mullet
fatias de Tomar sponge slices served in a light syrup

fatias douradas slices of bread dipped in egg, fried and covered with sugar and cinnamon, French toast
favada à portuguesa broad beans cooked with smoked meats, onions and coriander
favas broad beans
febras thin slices of fried pork
febras de porco à alentejana pork fillet with onions, **chouriço** and bacon
feijão encarnado red beans
feijão frade black-eyed beans
feijão guisado beans stewed with bacon in a tomato sauce
feijão preto black beans
feijão verde cozido boiled French beans
feijoada bean stew with pork meat and **chouriço**
fígado de coentrada pork liver with coriander
fígado de galinha chicken liver
fígado de porco de cebolada pork liver with onions
filetes de pescada hake fillet in batter
folhados de carne meat puff-pastries
frango young chicken
frango à piri-piri barbecued chicken with or without chilli
frango assado roast tender chicken
fresco/a cold or fresh
fressura de porco guisada pork offal casserole
fricassé meat or fish (generally chicken) served with an egg and lemon sauce
frio cold

fritada de peixe an assortment of deep-fried fish
frito/a fried
fumado/a smoked
fundo de alcachofra artichoke heart
galinhola woodcock
gambas large prawns
gambas na chapa large prawns cooked on the hot plate
garoto small white coffee
gasosa fizzy drink
gaspacho cold soup with finely cut vegetables
gelo ice
gim gin
ginjinha morello-cherry liqueur typical of Portugal
girafa litre glass of beer
granizado de café iced coffee
grelhado grilled
guisado stewed
hortaliça generic name given to vegetables
hortelã mint
hortelã-pimenta peppermint
imperial small glass of beer
incluído included
inhame yam
iscas traditional pork liver dish with wine and garlic
...à jardineira garden-style with vegetables such as green beans and carrots
jardineira mixed vegetables
jarro carafe
javali wild boar

jeropiga fortified dessert wine
...à lagareiro baked dish made with lots of olive oil
lagostim-do-rio freshwater crayfish
lampreia lamprey (an eel-like fish)
lanche afternoon snack consisting of tea and cakes or buttered toast
lapas limpets, popular in Madeira and the Azores
lapas Afonso limpets served with an onion sauce
laranja descascada peeled orange, normally served with a sprinkle of sugar
laranjada fizzy orange
laranjada engarrafada bottled orange juice
lavagante species of lobster
leite-creme crème brûlée
licor de leite milk liqueur
licor de tangerina mandarin liqueur
língua estufada braised tongue
linguiça pork sausage with paprika
lista dos vinhos wine list
lombinho de porco pork loin
lombo de porco pork fillet
louro bay leaf
lulas à Algarvia squid in garlic, Algarve style
lulas guisadas stewed squid
lulas recheadas squid stuffed with garlic, onion, **chouriço** and squid tentacles
maçã assada large baked russet apple
macarrão macaroni
macedónia de frutas mixed fruit salad
malagueta hot pepper

mal passado rare
manjar celeste sweet made with eggs, breadcrumbs, almonds and sugar
mãozinhas de vitela guisadas stewed calves' feet
marinado/a marinated
...à marinheira with white wine, onions and parsley
marisqueira a restaurant or bar specialising in shellfish
marmelada quince jam – excellent with cheese
marmelo quince, a popular fruit, often baked
medalhão medallion
medronheira strawberry-tree fruit liqueur
meia-dose half-portion
meia garrafa half bottle
meio-doce medium-sweet
meio-seco medium-dry
mel de cana molasses
merenda afternoon snack
merendinha pastry filled with **chouriço** or **presunto** (ham)
mero red grouper fish
migas bread cooked with well-seasoned ingredients to form a kind of omelette
migas à alentejana thick bread soup with pork and garlic
migas de pão de milho thick maize bread soup with olive oil and garlic
mil-folhas millefeuille (custard pastry)

miolos brains
misto mixed
molho de caril curry sauce
molho de escabeche a sauce containing vinegar, normally served with cold fried fish
morcela spicy black pudding
morgado de figo dried pressed figs with spices
moscatel de Setúbal medium-sweet muscat wine
nabiça turnip greens
...na brasa char-grilled
...na cataplana stewed in a **cataplana** (typical double-wok pot used in the Alentejo and Algarve)
...na frigideira sautéed or fried
nata batida whipped cream
...no espeto kebab/on the spit
...no forno roasted or cooked in the oven
omeleta de cogumelos mushroom omelette
omeleta de fiambre ham omelette
omeleta simples plain omelette
ostras oysters
ouriço-do-mar sea-urchin
ovas fish roe
ovos cozidos boiled eggs
ovos escalfados poached eggs
ovos estrelados fried eggs
ovos mexidos scrambled eggs
paio thick smoked sausage made with lean meat
palha de Abrantes sweet made with eggs
panados slices of meat coated in egg and breadcrumbs and fried

pão de centeio rye bread
pão de forma bread for toast
pão de ló light sponge cake
pão de milho maize bread
pão de queijo Brazilian cheese and maize snack
pão saloio country-style bread
papas polenta soup
papas de milho doces sweet polenta
papos de anjo small egg cakes with syrup
pargo red bream
parrilhada grilled fish
pastéis tarts, cakes, pasties
pastéis de bacalhau salt cod cakes
pastéis de carne meat pasties
pastéis de feijão tarts made with beans, eggs and almonds
pastel de massa tenra meat pasty
pataniscas (de bacalhau) salt cod fritters
paté de fígado liver pâté
pé de porco com feijão pigs' trotters with beans
peixe assado/cozido/frito/grelhado baked/poached/fried/grilled fish
peixe e marisco fish and shellfish
peixe espada scabbard fish
peixe-galo John Dory
peixinhos da horta French beans fried in batter
pequeno almoço breakfast
percebes rock barnacles, highly prized shellfish
pescada com todos hake poached with potatoes and vegetables, served with a boiled egg

petisco savoury or snack
pezinhos de porco de coentrada pork trotters with coriander and garlic
picante spicy
pimenta pepper (spice)
pinhão pine kernel
pinhoada pinenut brittle
porco à alentejana traditional dish with pork, clams and herbs
porco assado roast pork
porco preta black pork
...à portuguesa with fried cubes of pork in garlic and olive oil
posta à mirandesa spit-roasted veal, Miranda-style
pouco picante mild
prato do dia dish of the day
prato principal main dish
pratos de carne meat dishes
prego steak roll
prego com fiambre steak and ham roll
prego no pão steak roll
prego no prato steak with fried egg and chips
presunto cured ham
preta dark
pudim Abade de Priscos rich egg pudding flavoured with port and lemon
pudim de bacalhau salt cod loaf served with tomato sauce
pudim de pão bread pudding

pudim de queijo cheese pudding
pudim de requeijão ricotta-type cheese pudding
pudim flan crème caramel
pudim Molotov egg-white pudding with egg sauce or caramel
queijadas de Évora cheese tarts made with ewes' milk cheese
queijadas de requeijão ricotta-type cheese tarts
queijinhos de amêndoa little almond sweets
queijinhos do céu egg yolk and sugar sweets
queijinhos frescos small curd cheeses
queijinhos secos small dried cheeses
queijo cabreiro goats' cheese
queijo cardiga cheese made from ewes' and goats' milk
queijo de cabra goats' cheese
queijo de ovelha small, dried ewes' milk cheeses
quente hot
rabanada french toast
raia skate
rancho a substantial soup of meat and chickpeas
recheado com... stuffed/filled with...
recheio stuffing
requeijão fresh curd cheese resembling ricotta
rim (rins) kidney
rissóis de camarão/peixe shrimp or fish rissoles
rojões crisp pieces of marinated pork
salada de feijão frade black-eyed bean salad, with boiled egg, olive oil and seasonings

salada de polvo a starter with cold octopus, seasoned with olive oil, coriander, onion and vinegar
salgados savouries (snacks)
salmão fumado smoked salmon
salmonetes grelhados grilled red mullet in a butter and lemon sauce
saloio small cheese made from ewes' or goats' milk, often served as a pre-starter
salpicão slices of large **chouriço**
salteado sautéed
sandes de lombo steak sandwich
sandes mista ham and cheese sandwich
santola spider crab
sapateira crab (generally dressed)
sardinhas assadas char-grilled sardines
sardinhas na telha oven-baked sardines cooked on a roof tile with olive oil and seasoning
seco/a dry
sericaia baked custard with cinnamon
serpa a type of ewes' milk cheese
serra a creamy cheese made from ewes' milk
serviço incluído service included
sidra cider
simples neat (as in 'neat whisky')
sonho fritter, dipped in sugar and cinnamon
sopa à alentejana soup Alentejo-style, made with chunks of bread, olive oil, fresh coriander and garlic, topped with poached egg
sopa de cabeça de peixe fish head soup with tomatoes, potatoes, stale bread and seasonings

sopa de camarão prawn soup
sopa de castanhas piladas hearty soup made with dried chestnuts, beans and rice
sopa de ervilhas pea soup
sopa de espinafres spinach soup
sopa de feijão bean soup with vegetables
sopa de grão chickpea soup
sopa de hortaliça vegetable soup
sopa de legumes vegetable soup
sopa de marisco shellfish soup
sopa de pedra a rich soup with lots of meat, beans and vegetables
sopa de rabo de boi oxtail soup
sopa do dia soup of the day
sopa dos campinos salt cod and tomato soup
sopa dourada dessert made with egg yolks
sopa seca thick bread soup with meat
suspiros meringues
tainha grey mullet
tarte de amêndoa almond tart
tarte de limão lemon tart
tarte de maçã apple tart
tasca/tasquinha small taverna traditionally serving cheap food and drink, although some have become gentrified and are no longer cheap
tempêro seasoning
tenro/a tender
tibornas slices of freshly baked bread sprinkled with coarse sea salt and olive oil
tigeladas de Abrantes individually baked custards

tisana herbal tea
tisana de camomila camomile tea
tisana de Lúcia-Lima vervaine tea
tornedó tournedos (of beef)
torradas toast
torta swiss roll
torta de laranja orange sponge roll
torta de Viana sponge roll filled with egg custard
tosta mista ham and cheese toasted sandwich
toucinho do céu egg and almond pudding
tremoços lupin seeds often eaten with beer
tripas à moda do Porto tripe stew with beans and various meats, Porto-style
trutas à moda do Minho trout cooked in wine and rich seasonings
truta de Barroso fried trout stuffed with ham
tutano marrow
vagens runner beans
variado assorted
vermute vermouth
(em) vinha d'alhos marinated in wine and garlic
vinho abafado locally made fortified wine
vinho adamado sweet wine
vinho da casa house wine
vinho espumante sparkling wine
vinho verde dry, sparkling 'green' wine made with slightly unripe grapes from the Minho region
vitela no espeto veal cooked on the spit
xerez sherry

Reference

Alphabet

The Portuguese alphabet is the same as the English. The letters K, W and Y are only used in foreign words that have come into use in Portuguese.

Como se escreve? **koh**-moo suh shkrev?	How do you spell it?
C de Carlos, L de Lisboa say duh **kar**loosh el duh leezh**boh**-uh	C for Carlos, L for Lisboa

A	ah	**Alexandre**	aluh-**shuñ**druh
B	bay	**Bastos**	**bash**-toosh
C	say	**Carlos**	**kar**loosh
D	day	**Daniel**	dan-**yel**
E	ay	**Eduardo**	eed**war**doo
F	ef	**França**	**fruñ**suh
G	zhay	**Gabriel**	gabree-**el**
H	a**gah**	**Holanda**	oh-**luñ**duh

I	ee	**Itália**	ee**tahl**-yuh
J	**zhot**uh	**José**	zhoo**ze**
K	**kah**puh	**kart**	karrt
L	el	**Lisboa**	leezh**boh**-uh
M	em	**Maria**	ma**ree**-uh
N	en	**Nicolau**	neekoo-**lah**-oo
O	oh	**Óscar**	**osh**kar
P	pay	**Paris**	pa**reesh**
Q	kay	**Quarto**	**kwar**too
R	err	**Ricardo**	ree**kar**doo
S	ess	**Susana**	soo**zan**uh
T	tay	**Teresa**	tuh-**ray**-zuh
U	oo	**Ulisses**	oo**lee**sush
V	vay	**Venezuela**	vuh-nuh-**zway**-luh
W	**duh**blioo	**WiFi**	wyfy
X	sheesh	**Xangai**	shuñg-**gy**
Y	eepsee**lohn**	**Youtube**	yootoob
Z	zay	**Zebra**	**zeb**ruh

Measurements and quantities

1 lb = approx. 0.5 kilo
1 pint = approx. 0.5 litre

Liquids

1/2 litre...	**meio litro de...** **may**oo **lee**troo duh...
a litre of...	**um litro de...** ooñ **lee**troo duh...
1/2 bottle of...	**meia garrafa de...** **may**uh ga**rrah**-fuh duh...
a bottle of...	**uma garrafa de...** **oo**muh ga**rrah**-fuh duh...
a glass of...	**um copo de...** ooñ **kop**oo duh...

Weights

100 grams of...	**cem gramas de...** sayñ **grah**-mush duh...
1/2 kilo of...	**meio quilo de...** **may**oo **kee**loo duh...
1 kilo of...	**um quilo de...** ooñ **kee**loo duh...

Food

a slice of...	**uma fatia de...** **oo**muh fa**tee**-uh duh...
a portion of...	**uma dose de...** **oo**muh **doh**-suh duh...
a dozen...	**uma dúzia de...** **oo**muh **doo**zee-uh duh...

a box of...	**uma caixa de...** **oo**muh **ky**-shuh duh...
a packet of...	**um pacote de...** ooñ pa**kot** duh...
a tin of...	**uma lata de...** **oo**muh **lah**-tuh duh...
a jar of...	**um boião de...** ooñ boy-**owñ** duh...

Miscellaneous

10 euros of...	**dez euros de...** desh **eur**oosh duh...
a half	**metade** muh-**tahd**
a quarter	**um quarto** ooñ **kwar**too
ten per cent	**dez por cento** desh poor **señ**too
more...	**mais...** mysh...
less...	**menos...** **meh**-noosh...
enough	**chega** **sheh**-guh
double	**o dobro** oo **doh**-broo
twice	**duas vezes** **doo**-ush **veh**-zush

Reference

three times **três vezes**
traysh **veh**-zush

Numbers

0 **zero** **zehr**-oo
1 **um (uma)** ooñ (**oo**muh)
2 **dois (duas)** doysh (**doo**-uz)
3 **três** traysh
4 **quatro** **kwat**roo
5 **cinco** **seeñ**koo
6 **seis** saysh
7 **sete** set
8 **oito** **oy**too
9 **nove** nov
10 **dez** desh
11 **onze** oñz
12 **doze** dohz
13 **treze** trezh
14 **catorze** ka**torz**
15 **quinze** keeñz
16 **dezasseis** dezuh-**saysh**
17 **dezassete** dezuh-**set**
18 **dezoito** de**zoy**too

Reference

19	**dezanove** dezuh-**nov**
20	**vinte** veeñt
21	**vinte e um** veeñtee-**ooñ**
22	**vinte e dois** veeñtee-**doysh**
23	**vinte e três** veeñtee-**traysh**
24	**vinte e quatro** veeñtee-**kwat**roo
25	**vinte e cinco** veeñtee-**seeñ**koo
26	**vinte e seis** veeñtee-**saysh**
27	**vinte e sete** veeñtee-**set**
28	**vinte e oito** veeñtee-**oy**too
29	**vinte e nove** veeñtee-**nov**
30	**trinta** **treeñ**tuh
40	**quarenta** kwa**reñ**tuh
50	**cinquenta** seeñ**kweñ**tuh
60	**sessenta** se**señ**tuh
70	**setenta** se**teñ**tuh
80	**oitenta** oy**teñ**tuh
90	**noventa** noo**veñ**tuh
100	**cem/cento** sayñ/**señ**too
110	**cento e dez** **señ**too ee desh
500	**quinhentos** keen-**yeñ**toosh
1,000	**mil** meel
2,000	**dois mil** doysh meel
1 million	**um milhão** ooñ meel-**yowñ**

1st	**primeiro** pree**may**roo	6th	**sexto** **sesh**-too
2nd	**segundo** se**goon**doo	7th	**sétimo** **set**eemoo
3rd	**terceiro** ter**say**roo	8th	**oitavo** oy**tah**-voo
4th	**quarto** **kwar**too	9th	**nono** **noh**-noo
5th	**quinto** **keeñ**too	10th	**décimo** **dess**eemoo

Days and months

Days

Monday	**segunda-feira**	se**goon**duh-**fay**ruh
Tuesday	**terça-feira**	**ter**suh-**fay**ruh
Wednesday	**quarta-feira**	**kwar**tuh-**fay**ruh
Thursday	**quinta-feira**	**keeñ**tuh-**fay**ruh
Friday	**sexta-feira**	**sesh**tuh-**fay**ruh
Saturday	**sábado**	**sah**-buh-doo
Sunday	**domingo**	do**meeñ**goo

Months

January	**janeiro**	zhuh**nay**roo
February	**fevereiro**	fuh-**vray**roo
March	**março**	**mar**soo
April	**abril**	a**breel**
May	**maio**	**my**-oo
June	**junho**	**zhoon**-yoo
July	**julho**	**zhool**-yoo
August	**agosto**	a**gosh**too
September	**setembro**	suh**teñ**broo
October	**outubro**	oh**too**broo
November	**novembro**	no**vayñ**-broo
December	**dezembro**	duh**zayñ**-broo

Seasons

spring	**a primavera**	uh preemuh-**vehr**uh
summer	**o verão**	oo vuh-**rowñ**
autumn	**o outono**	oo oh**toh**noo
winter	**o inverno**	oo eeñ**vehr**noo

What is today's date? **Qual é a data hoje?**
kwal e uh **dah**-tuh ohzh?

It's the 5th of May 2016 **É cinco de maio de dois mil e dezasseis**
e **seeñ**koo duh **my**-oo duh doysh meel ee dezuh-**saysh**

on Saturday **no sábado**
noo **sah**-buh-doo

on Saturdays	**aos sábados** awsh **sah**-buh-doosh
every Saturday	**todos os sábados** **toh**-doosh oosh **sah**-buh-doosh
this Saturday	**este sábado** esht **sah**-buh-doo
next Saturday	**o próximo sábado** oo **pross**eemoo **sah**-buh-doo
last Saturday	**o sábado passado** oo **sah**-buh-doo puh-**sah**-doo
in June	**em junho** ayñ **zhoon**-yoo
at the beginning of...	**no princípio de...** noo preeñ-**seep**-yoo duh...
at the end of...	**no fim de...** noo feeñ duh...
before the summer	**antes do verão** uñtsh doo vuh-**rowñ**
during the summer	**durante o verão** doo**ruñt** oo vuh-**rowñ**
after the summer	**depois do verão** duh-**poysh** doo vuh-**rowñ**

Time

The 24-hour clock is used a lot more than in Britain. After 1200 midday, it continues: **1300 – treze horas**, **1400 – catorze horas**, **1500 – quinze horas**, etc., until **2400 - vinte e quatro horas (meia-noite)**. With the 24-hour clock, the words **quarto** (quarter) and **meia** (half) aren't used:

1315 (1.15 p.m.)	**treze e quinze**
1930 (7.30 p.m.)	**dezanove e trinta**
2245 (10.45 p.m.)	**vinte e duas e quarenta e cinco**

What time is it?	**Que horas são?** kee **or**ush sowñ?
a.m./p.m.	**da manhã/da tarde** duh mun-**yañ**/duh tard
It's...	**São...** sowñ...
2 o'clock	**duas horas** **doo**-uz **or**ush
3 o'clock (etc.)	**três horas** trayz **or**ush
It's 1 o'clock	**É uma hora** e **oo**muh **or**uh
It's 1200 midday	**É meio-dia** e **may**oo **dee**-uh
At midnight	**À meia-noite** a **may**uh noyt
9	**nove horas** no**vee or**ush
9.10	**nove e dez** no**vee** desh
9.15	**nove e um quarto** no**vee** ooñ **kwar**too

Reference

9.20	**nove e vinte** no**vee** veeñt
9.30	**nove e trinta/nove e meia** no**vee treeñ**tuh/no**vee may**uh
9.35	**nove e trinta e cinco/ vinte e cinco para as dez** no**vee treeñ**tuh ee **seeñ**koo/ veeñ**tee seeñ**koo **pa**ruh ush desh
9.45	**dez menos um quarto/ nove e quarenta e cinco** desh **meh**-nooz ooñ **kwar**too/ no**vee** kwa**reñ**tuh ee **seeñ**koo
9.50	**dez para as dez/ nove e cinquenta** desh **pa**ruh ush desh/ no**vee** seeñk**weñ**tuh

Time phrases

When does it open/close?	**Quando abre/fecha?** **kwuñ**doo **ah**-bruh/**fay**shuh?
When does it begin/finish?	**Quando começa/acaba?** **kwuñ**doo koo**mess**uh/a**kah**-buh?
at 3 o'clock	**às três horas** ash trayz **or**ush
before 3 o'clock	**antes das três** uñtsh dush tresh
after 3 o'clock	**depois das três** duh-**poysh** dush tresh

Reference

today	**hoje** ohzh
tonight	**esta noite** **esh**tuh noyt
tomorrow	**amanhã** amun-**yuñ**
yesterday	**ontem** **oñ**tayñ

Public holidays

Unlike the UK, public holidays in Portugal are always on the given date (even if they fall on a Sunday).

January 1	**Ano Novo** New Year's Day
March/April	**Sexta-Feira Santa** Good Friday
March/April	**Páscoa** Easter Sunday
April 25	**Dia da Liberdade** Freedom Day
May 1	**Dia do Trabalhador** Labour Day
June 10	**Dia de Portugal** Portugal Day
August 15	**Assunção** Assumption of Mary
December 8	**Imaculada Conceição de Maria** Immaculate Conception of Mary
December 25	**Natal** Christmas Day

Phonetic map

When travelling in Portugal, you will need to bear in mind that place names as we know them are not necessarily the same in Portuguese. Imagine if you wanted to buy tickets at a train station but couldn't see your destination on the departures list! This handy map eliminates such problems by indicating the locations and local pronunciations of major towns and cities.

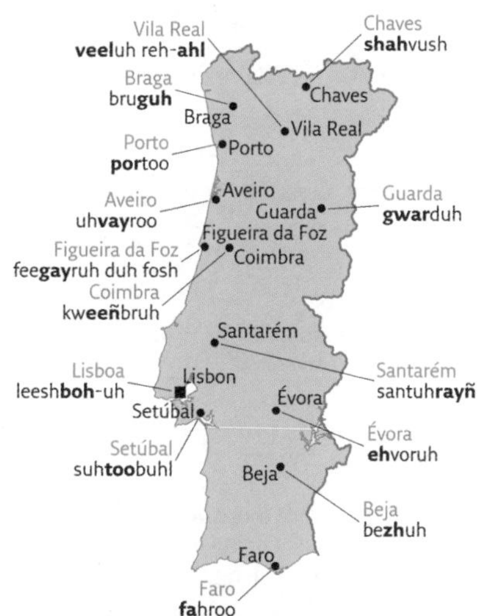

Grammar

Nouns

Portuguese nouns are masculine or feminine, and their gender is shown by the words for 'the' (**o/a**) and 'a' (**um/uma**) used before them (articles):

	masculine	feminine
singular	**o castelo** the castle	**a mesa** the table
	um castelo a castle	**uma mesa** a table
plural	**os castelos** the castles	**as mesas** the tables
	(uns) castelos (some) castles	**(umas) mesas** (some) tables

Nouns ending in -**o** or -**or** are usually masculine. Those ending in -**a**, -**agem**, -**dade** and -**tude** tend to be feminine. Nouns ending in a vowel form the plural by adding -**s**, while those ending in a consonant usually add -**es**. Words ending in -**m** change to -**ns**, and words ending in -**l**, change to -**is**.

Note: When used after the words **a** (to), **de** (of), **em** (in) and **por** (by), articles (and many other words) contract:

a + **as** = **às** ash	to the
de + **um** = **dum** dooñ	of a
em + **uma** = **numa** **noo**-muh	to a
por + **os** = **pelos** **peh**-loosh	by the

This, that, these, those...

These depend on the gender and number of the noun they represent:

este rapaz this boy	**esta rapariga** this girl
estes rapazes these boys	**estas raparigas** these girls
esse rapaz that boy	**essa rapariga** that girl
esses rapazes those boys	**essas raparigas** those girls
aquele rapaz that boy (over there)	**aquela rapariga** that girl (over there)
aqueles rapazes those boys (over there)	**aquelas raparigas** those girls (over there)

Adjectives

Portuguese adjectives normally follow the nouns they describe and reflect the gender in e.g. **a maçã verde** the green apple. The exceptions are **bom** (good) and **grande** (great, big) which can go before the noun.

To make an adjective feminine, -**o** endings change to -**a**, and -**or** and -**ês** change to -**ora** and -**esa**. Otherwise they generally have the same form for both genders.

masculine		feminine	
the red book	**o livro vermelho**	the red skirt	**a saia vermelha**
the talkative man	**o homem falador**	the talkative woman	**a mulher faladora**

To make adjectives plural, follow the rules given for nouns.

My, your, his, her...

These words depend on the gender and number of the noun and not the sex of the 'owner'.

	with masc./fem.	with plural nouns
my	**o meu/a minha**	**os meus/as minhas**
his/her/ its/your	**o seu/a sua**	**os seus/as suas**
our	**o nosso/a nossa**	**os nossos/as nossas**
your	**o vosso/a vossa**	**os vossos/as vossas**
their/ your	**o seu/a sua**	**os seus/as suas**

Note: Since **o seu**, **a sua**, etc. can mean 'his', 'her', 'your', etc., the words **dele**, **dela**, **deles** and **delas** are often used to avoid confusion:

os livros dela	her books
os livros deles	their books

Pronouns

subject		object	
I	**eu** **ay**-oo	me	**me** muh
you (informal)	**tu** too	you (informal)	**te** teh
you	**você** voh-**say**	you	**o/a** oo/uh
he	**ele** ayl	him	**o** oo
she	**ela** **ay**luh	her	**a** uh
it	**ele/ela** ayl/**ay**luh	it	**o/a** oo/uh
we	**nós** nosh	us	**nos** noosh
you	**vós** vosh	you	**vos** voosh
they (masc.)	**eles** **ay**lush	them (masc.)	**os** oosh
they (fem.)	**elas** **el**ush	them (fem.)	**as** ush
you (informal)	**vocês** voh-**saysh**	you (informal)	**os/as** oosh/ush

Notes

1. Use of 'you': The polite way of addressing someone would be with **o senhor** or **a senhora**, using the (s)he form of the verb and the object pronoun **o/a**. The semi-formal 'you' is **você**, however some people dislike **você** and

Grammar

consider it slightly coarse. An alternative semi-formal way of addressing someone is to use the 'he/she/it' form of the verb, plus the person's name, e.g. **A Laura vem a Portugal?** Are you coming to Portugal, Laura? The the informal 'you' is **tu** (as in French).

2. Subject pronouns are normally not used except for emphasis or to avoid confusion:

   eu vou para Lisboa e ele vai para Coimbra
   I'm going to Lisbon and he's going to Coimbra

3. Object pronouns are usually placed after the verb and joined with a hyphen:

   vejo-o I see him

   However, in sentences beginning with a 'question' or 'negative' word, the pronoun goes in front of the verb:

   quando o viu? when did you see him?
   não o vi I did not see him

   In phrases beginning with 'that', 'who', etc. (subordinate clauses), the pronoun also precedes the verb:

   sei que o viu I know that you saw him
   o homem que o viu the man who saw him

4. Use of 'me': **me** = to me and **nos** = to us, but **lhe** = to him/to her/to it/to you (formal), **te** = to you (informal), **vos** = to you (plural) and **lhes** = to them/to you.

Verbs

Portuguese regular verbs follow one of three patterns of endings. Examples of the present and past tenses are given overleaf.

Present tense

Verbs ending in -**ar**

cantar	**to sing**
canto	I sing
cantas	you sing
canta	(s)he/it sings/you sing
cantamos	we sing
cantais	you sing
cantam	they/you sing

Verbs ending in -**er**

comer	**to eat**
como	I eat
comes	you eat
come	(s)he/it eats/you eat
comemos	we eat
comeis	you eat
comem	they/you eat

Verbs ending in -**ir**

partir	**to leave**
parto	I leave
partes	you leave
parte	(s)he/it leaves/you leave
partimos	we leave
partis	you leave
partem	they/you leave

Past tense

Verbs ending in -**ar**

cantar	**to sing**
cantei	I sang
cantaste	you sang
cantou	(s)he/it/you sang
cantámos	we sang
cantastes	you sang
cantaram	they/you sang

Grammar

Verbs ending in -**er**

comer	**to eat**
comi	I ate
comeste	you ate
comeu	(s)he/it/you ate
comemos	we ate
comestes	you ate
comeram	they/you ate

Verbs ending in -**ir**

partir	**to leave**
parti	I left
partiste	you left
partiu	(s)he/it/you left
partimos	we left
partistes	you left
partiram	they/you left

Irregular verbs don't follow a pattern, so you need to learn their endings. Four of the most common verbs are irregular:

ser	**to be**
sou	I am
és	you are
é	(s)he/it is/you are
somos	we are
sois	you are
são	they/you are

estar	**to be**
estou	I am
estás	you are
está	(s)he/it is/you are
estamos	we are
estais	you are
estão	they/you are

ter	**to have**
tenho	I have
tens	you have
tem	(s)he/it has/you have
temos	we have
tendes	you have
têm	they/you have

ir	**to go**
vou	I go
vais	you go
vai	(s)he/it goes/you go
vamos	we go
ides	you go
vão	they/you go

Note: **Ser** and **estar** both mean 'to be'.

Ser is used to describe a permanent place or state:

sou inglês	I am English
é uma praia	it is a beach

Estar is used to describe a temporary state or where something is located:

como está?	how are you?
onde está o livro?	where is the book?

A

a	um (uma)	**ooñ** (**oo**muh)
able: ***to be able (to)***	poder	poo**dehr**
about (roughly)	mais ou menos	mysh oh **meh**-noosh
about ten o'clock	por volta das dez	poor voltuh dush desh
above	acima de	uh-**see**-muh duh
to accept	aceitar	uh-say**tar**
(approve of)	aprovar	uh-proo**var**
access	o acesso	uh-**sess**oo
accident	o acidente	asee**deñt**
accommodation	o alojamento	alozhuh-**meñ**to
account (bill)	a conta	**koñ**tuh
(in bank)	a conta bancária	**koñ**tuh buñ**kar**-yuh
to ache	doer	doo-**ehr**
my head aches	dói-me a cabeça	**doy**-muh uh kuh-**beh**-suh
address	a morada	moo-**rah**-duh
admission charge/fee	o preço de entrada	**pray**-soo duh eñ-**trah**-duh
adult	o/a adulto(a)	uh**dool**too(uh)
advance: ***in advance***	antecipadamente	uñtessee-pah-duh-**meñt**
aeroplane	o avião	av-**yowñ**
afraid: ***to be afraid of***	ter medo de	tehr **meh**-doo duh
after	depois	duh-**poysh**
afternoon	a tarde	tard
again	outra vez	**oh**-truh vesh
age	a idade	ee**dahd**
agency	a agência	uh-**zhayñ**-syuh
ago: 2 ***days ago***	há 2 dias	a doysh **dee**-ush
to agree	concordar	koñkor**dar**
AIDS	a SIDA	**see**duh
air conditioning	o ar condicionado	ar koñdeess-yoo**nah**-doo
airline	a linha aérea	**leen**-yuh ah-**ehr**eh-uh
airport	o aeroporto	ayroo-**por**too
air ticket	o bilhete de avião	beel-**yet** duh av-**yowñ**

A

English - Portuguese

alarm	o alarme	a**lar**muh
alarm clock	o despertador	deesh-pehrtuh-**dor**
alcohol	o álcool	**ahl**kol
alcohol-free	sem álcool	sayñ **ahl**kol
alcoholic adj	alcoólico(a)	al-**ko**leekoo(uh)
all	todo(a), todos(as)	**toh**-doo(uh), **toh**-doosh(ush)
allergic	alérgico(a)	a**lehr**-zheekoo(uh)
I'm allergic to	sou alérgico(a) a	soh a**lehr**-zheekoo(uh) uh
to allow	permitir	pehr-meet**eer**
to be allowed (to)	ter permissão (para)	tehr puhrmis**sowñ** (pa**ruh**)
all right	está bem	shta bayñ
are you all right?	você está bem?	voh-**say** shta bayñ?
almost	quase	**kwah**-zuh
alone	sozinho(a)	soh-**zeen**-yoo(uh)
already	já	zhah
also	também	tuñ**bayñ**
always	sempre	**sayñ**pruh
a.m.	da manhã	duh mun-**yañ**
ambulance	a ambulância	amboo**luñss**-yuh
amount: ***total amount***	o total	too-**tahl**
and	e	ee
angry	zangado(a)	zuñ**gah**doo(uh)
animal	o animal	aneem**ahl**
to announce	anunciar	anoonsee**ar**
another	um(a) outro(a)	ooñ **oh**-troo(truh)
answer n	a resposta	resh-**posh**tuh
to answer	responder	resh-pon**dehr**
antibiotic	o antibiótico	uñteebee**oh**-teekoo
antihistamine	o anti-histamínico	uñtee-eestuh-**mee**neekoo
anti-inflammatory	o anti-inflamatório	uñtee-eeñfluh-muh-**tor**yoo
antiseptic	o antissético	uñtee**se**-teekoo
any (some)	algum(a)	al**gooñ**/al**goo**muh
(negative)	nenhum(a)	nayn-**yooñ**/nayn-**yoo**muh

anyone (in questions)	alguém	al**gayñ**
(negative)	ninguém	neeñ**gayñ**
anything (in questions)	alguma coisa	al**goo**muh **koy**-zuh
(negative)	nada	**nah**-duh
apartment	o apartamento	uh-partuh-**meñ**too
apple	a maçã	muh-**sañ**
appointment (meeting)	o encontro	ayñ-**koñ**troo
(doctor)	a consulta	koñ**sool**tuh
approximately	aproximadamente	a**pross**ee-mah-duh-**meñt**
arm	o braço	**brah**-soo
arrival	a chegada	shuh-**gah**-duh
to arrive	chegar	shuh-**gar**
to ask (question)	perguntar	pehr-goon**tar**
(to ask for something)	pedir	ped**eer**
aspirin	a aspirina	ashpee**ree**nuh
asthma	a asma	**ash**muh
I have asthma	tenho asma	**ten**-yoo **ash**muh
at	em; a	ayñ; uh
at 8 o'clock	às oito	ash **oy**too
at night	à noite	a noyt
ATM	Multibanco®	mooltee-**buñ**koo
attractive (person)	atraente	atrah-**eñt**
automatic	automático(a)	owto**mah**-teekoo(uh)
available	disponível	deesh-poh-**nee**-vel
to avoid	evitar	eh-vee**tar**
awful	terrível	teh-**rree**vel

B

baby	o bebé	be-**be**
baby's bottle	o biberão	bee-bay**rowñ**
baby seat (in car)	a cadeira de bebé	kuh**day**ruh duh be-**be**
back (of body)	as costas	ush **cosh**-tush
bad (weather, news)	mau (má)	mow (mah)
(fruit, vegetables)	podre	**pod**ruh
bag	o saco	**sah**-koo
(case)	a mala	**mah**-luh

baggage	a bagagem	buh-**gah**-zhayñ
ball	a bola	**boh**-luh
bank	o banco	**buñ**koo
bank account	a conta bancária	**koñ**tuh buñ**kar**-yuh
bar	o bar	bar
barbecue	o churrasco	shoo**rrash**koo
basement	a cave	kahv
bath	a banheira	bun**yay**ruh
bathroom	a casa de banho	**kah**-zuh duh **bun**-yoo
battery (for car)	a bateria	batuh-**ree**-uh
(torch, radio, etc.)	a pilha	**peel**yuh
B&B	o quarto com pequeno-almoço	**kwar**too koñ puh-**kay**noo-al**moh**-soo
(place)	a pensão	payñ-**sowñ**
to be	ser; estar	sehr; esh-**tar**
beach	a praia	**pry**-uh
beautiful	belo(a); lindo(a)	**beh**-loo(uh); **leeñ**doo(uh)
because	porque	**poor**kuh
to become	tornar-se	tor**nar**-suh
bed	a cama	**kah**-muh
bedroom	o quarto	**kwar**too
beef	a carne de vaca	karn duh**vah**-kuh
beer	a cerveja	ser**vay**-zhuh
before	antes (de)	uñtsh (duh)
to begin	começar	koome**ssar**
behind	atrás (de)	uh-**truz** (duh)
to believe	acreditar	uh-krehdee**tar**
to belong to	pertencer a	pehrtayñ**sehr** a
below	debaixo (de)	duh-**by**shoo (duh)
(less than)	abaixo (de)	a**by**shoo (duh)
beside (next to)	ao lado (de)	ow **lah**-doo (duh)
best: ***the best***	o/a melhor	mel-**yor**
better (than)	melhor (do que)	mel-**yor** (doo kuh)
between	entre	**ayñ**truh
to beware of	ter cuidado com	tehr kwee**dah**-doo koñ
bicycle	a bicicleta	beesee**klay**tuh
big	grande	gruñd

bigger (than)	maior (que)	may**or** (kuh)
bill (in hotel, restaurant)	a conta	**koñ**tuh
(for work done)	a fatura	fa**too**ruh
(gas, telephone)	a conta	**koñ**tuh
birthday	o aniversário	aneever**sar**yoo
happy birthday	parabéns	paruh-**baynsh**
biscuits	as bolachas	ush boo**lash**ush
bit: ***a bit (of)***	um bocado (de)	ooñ boo**kah**doo (duh)
to bite (animal)	morder	moor**dehr**
(insect)	picar	pee**kar**
bitten (by animal)	mordido(a)	moor**dee**doo(uh)
(by insect)	picado(a)	pee**kah**doo
black	preto(a)	**preh**-too(uh)
to bleed	sangrar	suñ-**grar**
blind (person)	cego(a)	**seh**-goo(uh)
blond (person)	louro(a)	**low**-roo(uh)
blood	o sangue	**suñg**
blood pressure	a tensão arterial	tayñ-sowñ artehr-**yahl**
blood test	a análise ao sangue	u**nah**-leezeeow **suñg**
blouse	a blusa	**bloo**zuh
blue	azul	a**zool**
to board (plane, train, etc.)	embarcar	ayñbar**kar**
boarding card	o cartão de embarque	kar**towñ** duh ayñ-**bark**
boat	barco	**bar**koo
body	o corpo	**kor**poo
book	o livro	**lee**vroo
to book	reservar	ruh-zer**var**
booking	a reserva	ruh-**zehr**vuh
booking office	a bilheteira	beel-ye**teh**ruh
bookshop	a livraria	leevruh-**ree**-uh
boots	as botas	ush **boh**tush
bottle	a garrafa	ga**rrah**-fuh
box	a caixa	**ky**-shuh
boy	o rapaz	ruh-**paysh**
boyfriend	o namorado	namoo-**rah**-doo
brandy	o brandy	**brañ**dee

bread	o pão	powñ
to break	partir	par**teer**
breakfast	o pequeno-almoço	puh-**kay**noo-al**moh**-soo
to breathe	respirar	resh-pee**rar**
bride	a noiva	**noy**vuh
bridegroom	o noivo	**noy**voo
bridge	a ponte	poñt
to bring	trazer	tra**zehr**
Britain	a Grã-Bretanha	grañ-bruh-**tun**-yuh
British	britânico(a)	bree**tun**eekoo
broken	partido(a)	par**tee**doo(uh)
broken down (car, etc.)	avariado(a)	avaree-**ah**-doo
bronchitis	a bronquite	broñ**keet**
brother	o irmão	eer**mowñ**
brown	castanho(a)	kash-**tun**-yoo(uh)
to build	construir	**koñsh**-troo-eer
bull	o touro	**toh**-roo
bullfight	a tourada	toh-**rah**-duh
bureau de change	a casa de câmbio	**kah**-zuh duh **kuñ**byoo
burger	o hambúrguer	añ**boor**gehr
to burn	queimar	kay**mar**
bus	o autocarro	owtoo-**karr**oo
bus pass	o passe de autocarro	pass duh owtoo-**karr**oo
bus station	a estação de autocarros	shtuh-**sowñ** duh owtoo-**karr**oosh
bus stop	a paragem de autocarros	pa**rah**-zhayñ duh owtoo-**karr**oosh
bus ticket	o bilhete de autocarro	beel-**yet** duh owtoo-**karr**oo
business	os negócios	oosh ne**goh**-seeoosh
on business	de/em negócios	duh/ayñ ne**goh**-seeoosh
business class	a classe executiva	klass ezeh-koo**tee**vuh
busy	ocupado(a)	okoo**pah**doo/uh
but	mas	mush
butter	a manteiga	muñ**tay**-guh

to buy	comprar	koñ**prar**
by	por	poor
(near)	perto (de)	**pehr**-too (duh)
(next to)	ao lado (de)	ow **lah**-doo (duh)
by bus	de autocarro	duh owtoo-**karr**oo
by train	de comboio	duh koñ**boy**oo

C

café	o café	kuh-**fe**
cake	o bolo	**boh**-loo
cake shop	a pastelaria	pash-teluh-**ree**-uh
to call	chamar	shuh-**mar**
call (telephone)	a chamada	shuh-**mah**-duh
camcorder	a camcorder	kuñ**kor**dehr
camera	a máquina fotográfica	**mak**eenuh foto**grah**-feekuh
to camp	acampar	uh-kuñ**par**
campsite	o parque de campismo	park duh kuñ**peesh**-moo
can (to be able)	poder	poo**dehr**
Canada	o Canadá	kuh-nuh-**dah**
Canadian	canadiano(a)	kuh-nuh-dy**uh**-noo(uh)
to cancel	cancelar	kuñsuh-**lar**
cancellation	o cancelamento	kuñsuhluh-**meñ**too
car	o carro	**karr**oo
car hire	o aluguer de automóveis	aloo**gehr** duh owtoo-**moh**-vaysh
car insurance	o seguro de automóveis	se**goo**roo duh owtoo-**moh**-vaysh
car park	o estaciona-mento	esh-tassyoonuh-**meñ**too
caravan	a caravana	karuh-**vun**uh
careful	cuidadoso(a)	kweeduh-**do**zoo
be careful!	cuidado!	kwee**dah**-doo!
carrot	a cenoura	suh-**noh**-ruh
to carry	transportar	truñspoor-**tar**
case (suitcase)	a mala	**mah**-luh
cash	o dinheiro	deen-**yay**-roo
to cash (cheque)	levantar	leh-vuñ**tar**

cash desk	a caixa	**ky**-shuh
cash machine	o Multibanco®	mooltee-**buñ**koo
castle	o castelo	kush-**te**loo
casualty department	o Serviço de Urgências	sehr-**vee**-soo duh oor-**zhayñ**-see-ush
cat	o gato	**gah**-too
to catch (bus, train, etc.)	apanhar	apun-**yar**
cathedral	a catedral	kuh-tuh-**drahl**
CD	o CD	see-**dee**
centimetre	o centímetro	sayñ-**tee**-metroo
central	central	sayñ-**trahl**
central heating	o aquecimento central	akuh-see**meñ**too sayñ-**trahl**
cent	o cêntimo	**sayñ**-tee-moo
centre	o centro	**señ**troo
cereal (breakfast)	os cereais	oosh suh-reh-**ysh**
chair	a cadeira	kuh-**day**-ruh
champagne	o champanhe	shuñ**pun**-yuh
change (coins)	o dinheiro trocado	deen-**yay**-roo troo**kah**-doo
(money returned)	o troco	**troh**-koo
to change	trocar; mudar	troo**kar**; moo**dar**
(clothes)	mudar de roupa	moo**dar** duh **roh**-puh
(train)	mudar	moo**dar**
to change money	trocar dinheiro	troo**kar** deen-**yay**-roo
changing room	o gabinete de provas	gubee-**net** duh **proh**-vush
charge	o custo	**koosh**-too
cover charge	o couvert	koo**vehr**
to charge	cobrar	ko**brar**
cheap	barato(a)	ba**rah**-too(uh)
to check	verificar	veh-ree-fee**kar**
to check in (at airport, hotel)	fazer o check-in	fa**zehr** oo check-in
check-in desk	o balcão do check-in	bal**kowñ** doo check-in
cheers!	saúde!	sah-**ood**!
cheese	o queijo	**kay**-zhoo

chef	o cozinheiro-chefe/a cozinheira-chefe	koo-zeen-**yay**roo-shef/koo-zeen-**yay**ruh-shef
chemist's	a farmácia	far**mass**-yuh
chicken	a galinha; o frango	ga**leen**-yuh; oo **fruñ**goo
child	a criança	kree-**uñ**suh
children	as crianças	ush kree-**uñ**sush
chilli	a malagueta	maluh-**ge**tuh
chips	as batatas fritas	ush bu**tah**-tush **free**-tush
chocolate	o chocolate	shoo-koo**laht**
to choose	escolher	eesh-kohl-**yer**
Christmas	o Natal	nuh-**tahl**
church	a igreja	ee**greh**zhuh
cigarette	o cigarro	see-**gah**-rroo
cinema	o cinema	see**neh**-muh
city	a cidade	see**dahd**
city centre	o centro (da cidade)	**señ**troo (duh see**dahd**)
class: ***first class***	primeira classe	pree**may**ruh klass
second class	segunda classe	suh**goon**-duh klass
clean	limpo(a)	**leeñ**poo(uh)
to clean	limpar	leeñ**par**
client	o/a cliente	klee-**eñt**
to climb	subir	soo-**beer**
clock	o relógio	ruh-**lozh**-yoo
to close	fechar	fuh-**shar**
closed	fechado(a)	fuh-**shah**-doo(uh)
clothes	as roupas	ush **roh**-push
clothes shop	a loja de roupa	**lo**zhuh duh **roh**-puh
cloudy	nublado(a)	noo**blah**-doo(uh)
coach	a camioneta	kuh-mee-oh-**neh**-tuh
coach station	a rodoviária	rodovee**ar**-yuh
coast	a costa	**kosh**-tuh
coat	o casaco	kuh-**zah**-koo
cod	o bacalhau	bah-kal-**yow**
coffee	o café	kuh-**fe**
coin	a moeda	**mway**-duh

cold	frio(a)	**free**-oo(uh)
it's cold	está frio	shta **free**-oo(uh)
cold (illness)	a constipação	koñ-steepuh-**sowñ**
to collect	colecionar	kolessyo**nar**
(to collect someone)	ir buscar	eer boosh-**kar**
colour	a cor	kor
to come	vir	veer
(arrive)	chegar	shuh**gar**
to come back	voltar	vol**tar**
to come in	entrar	ayñ**trar**
come in!	entre!	**ayñ**-tree!
comfortable	confortável	koñfort**ah**-vel
company (firm)	empresa	eñ**preh**-zuh
to complain	queixar-se (de)	kay-**shar**-suh (duh)
complaint	a queixa	**kay**-shuh
complete	completo(a)	koñ**pleh**-too(uh)
to complete	completar	koñplay**tar**
computer	o computador	koñpootuh-**dor**
concert	o concerto	koñ**sehr**-too
concession	a concessão	koñsuh-**sowñ**
condom	o preservativo	prehzervuh-**tee**voo
conference	a conferência	koñfeh-**rayñ**-syuh
to confirm	confirmar	koñfeer**mar**
confirmation (of booking)	a confirmação	koñfeermuh-**sowñ**
congratulations!	parabéns!	paruh-**baynsh**!
connection (flight, etc.)	a ligação	lee-guh-**sowñ**
consulate	o consulado	koñsoo**lah**-doo
to consult	consultar	koñsool**tar**
to contact	pôr-se em contacto com	por se ayñ koñ**tak**too koñ
contact lenses	as lentes de contacto	ush leñtsh duh koñ**tak**too
to continue	continuar	koñteen**war**
contraception	contraceção	koñtruhses**sowñ**
convenient: ***is it convenient?***	é conveniente?	e koñveh-nee-**eñt**?
to cook	cozinhar	kozeen-**yar**
cool	fresco(a)	**fresh**-koo(uh)

to copy	copiar	koopee**ar**
corner	o canto	**kuñ**too
corridor	o corredor	koo-rre**dor**
to cost	custar	koosh**tar**
cot	o berço	**behr**-soo
to cough	tossir	too-**seer**
cough	a tosse	toss
country	o país	pah-**eesh**
countryside	o campo	**kuñ**poo
couple (2 people)	o casal	kuh-**zahl**
a couple of...	um par de	ooñ **par** duh
course (of meal)	o prato	**prah**-too
(of study)	o curso	**koor**-soo
cover charge	o couvert	koo-**vehr**
crash (car)	o choque	**shok**
to crash	colidir	kolee-**deer**
cream (face, etc.)	o creme	krem
(on milk)	a nata	**nah**-tuh
credit card	o cartão de crédito	kar**towñ** duh **kred**eetoo
crime	o crime	**kree**muh
crisps	as batatas fritas	ush bu**tah**-tush **free**tush
to cross (road)	atravessar	uhtruvuh**ssar**
crossroads	o cruzamento	kroozuh-**meñ**too
crowded	cheio(a) de gente	**shay**oo(uh) duh zheñt
to cry (weep)	chorar	shoo**rar**
cucumber	o pepino	pee**pee**noo
cup	a chávena	**shah**-veh-nuh
currency	a moeda	**mway**-duh
customer	o freguês/a freguesa	fre**gaysh**/fre**gay**zuh
customs (at airport etc.)	a alfândega	al**fuñ**duh-guh
customs declaration	a declaração alfandegária	deh-klaruh-**sowñ** alfuñduh-**gar**-yuh
to cut	cortar	kor**tar**
cut	o corte	kort
cut and blow-dry	cortar e secar	kor**tar** ee seh-**kar**

D

daily	cada dia	**kah**-duh **dee**-uh
dairy produce	os laticínios	oosh lah-tee-**see**-nee-oosh
damage	os danos	oosh **dah**-noosh
danger	o perigo	peh-**ree**goo
dangerous	perigoso(a)	peh-ree**go**zoo(uh)
dark	o escuro	esh-**koo**-roo
adj	escuro(a)	esh-**koo**-roo(uh)
date	a data	**dah**-tuh
date of birth	a data de nascimento	**dah**-tuh duh nashee-**meñ**too
daughter	a filha	**feel**-yuh
day	o dia	**dee**-uh
every day	todos os dias	**toh**-doosh oosh **dee**-ush
per day	por dia	poor **dee**-uh
deaf	surdo(a)	**soor**-doo(uh)
death	a morte	mort
debt	a dívida	**dee**-veeduh
to declare: ***nothing to declare***	nada a declarar	**nah**-duh uh dekla**rar**
deep	fundo(a)	**foon**-doo(uh)
delay	a demora	deh-**mor**-uh
delayed	atrasado(a)	atruh-**zah**-doo(uh)
dentist	o/a dentista	deñ**teesh**tuh
deodorant	o desodorizante	deh-zodoree-**zuñt**
to depart	partir	par**teer**
departure lounge	a sala de embarque	**sah**-luh duh ayñ-**bark**
departures	as partidas	ush par-**tee**-dush
deposit	o depósito	duh-**poz**eetoo
to describe	descrever	desh-kreh-**vehr**
desk	a secretária	suh-kreh-**tar**-yuh
(in hotel, airport)	o balcão	bal**kowñ**
dessert	a sobremesa	sobruh-**may**-zuh
details	os pormenores	poor-meh-**nor**-ush
to develop	desenvolver	dezeñvol**vehr**

diabetic (person)	diabético(a)	dee-uh-**bet**eekoo(kuh)
to dial	marcar	mar**kar**
dialling code	o código	**ko**deegoo
to die	morrer	moo-**rrehr**
diesel	o gasóleo	ga**zol**-yoo
diet	a dieta	dee-**eh**tuh
I'm on a diet	estou de dieta	shto duh dee-**eh**tuh
different	diferente	dee-fe**reñt**
difficult	difícil	dee**fee**seel
digital camera	máquina fotográfica digital	**mak**eenuh foto**grah**-feekuh deezhee-**tahl**
dining room	a sala de jantar	**sah**-luh duh zhuñ**tar**
dinner	o jantar	zhuñ**tar**
direct	direto(a)	dee**re**too(uh)
directions (instructions)	instruções	eeñstroos-**oyñsh**
directory (phone)	a lista telefónica	**leesh**tuh tuh-luh-**fo**neekuh
dirty	sujo(a)	**soo**-zhoo(uh)
disabled	deficiente	duh-feess-**yeñt**
disabled person	o/a deficiente	duh-feess-**yeñt**
to disagree	discordar	deesh-kor**dar**
to disappear	desaparecer	dezuh-pare**ssehr**
disappointed	desiludido(a)	dee-zee-loo-**dee**-doo(uh)
disco	a discoteca	deesh-ko**teh**-kuh
discount	o desconto	deesh**koñ**too
to discover	descobrir	deeshkoo**breer**
disease	a doença	doo-**eñ**suh
distance	a distância	deesh-**tuñss**-yuh
to disturb	incomodar	eeñkomo**dar**
diversion	o desvio	deesh-**vee**-oo
divorced	divorciado(a)	deevoors-**yah**-doo(uh)
dizzy	tonto(a)	**toñ**-too(uh)
to do	fazer	fa**zehr**
doctor	o/a médico(a)	**med**eekoo(uh)
documents	os documentos	dokoo**meñ**toosh
dog (male)	o cão	kowñ
(female)	a cadela	kuh-**deh**-luh

dollar	o dólar	**do**lur
door	a porta	**por**tuh
double	o dobro	**do**broo
double bed	a cama de casal	**kah**-muh duh kuh-**zahl**
double room	o quarto duplo	**kwar**too **doo**-ploo
down: *to go down*	descer	desh-**sehr**
draught (of air)	a corrente de ar	koo-**rreñt** duh ar
draught lager	a imperial	eeñpehr-**yahl**
dress	o vestido	veesh-**tee**doo
to dress (oneself)	vestir-se	veesh-**teer**-suh
dressing (for food)	o tempero; o molho	tayñ**pe**roo; **mol**-yoo
(for wound)	o penso	**payñ**-soo
drink	a bebida	beh-**bee**-duh
to drink	beber	beh-**behr**
drinking water	a água potável	**ahg**-wuh poo**tah**-vel
to drive	conduzir	koñdoo**zeer**
driver	o/a condutor(a)	koñdoo**tor**(uh)
driving licence	a carta de condução	**kar**tuh duh koñdoo**sowñ**
to drown	afogar	afoo-**gar**
drug (medicine)	o medicamento	**med**eekuh-**meñ**too
(narcotic)	a droga	**dro**guh
drunk	bêbedo(a)	**bay**-beh-doo(uh)
dry	seco(a)	**seh**-koo(uh)
to dry	secar	seh-**kar**
dryer	o secador	seh-kuh-**dor**
during	durante	doo**ruñt**
duty (tax)	o imposto	eeñ**posh**-too
duty-free	livre de impostos	**lee**-vree duh eeñ**posh**-toosh

E

each	cada	**kah**-duh
ear	a orelha	oo-**rel**-yuh
earache	a dor de ouvidos	dor duh oh-**vee**doosh
early	cedo	**seh**-doo
east	o leste	laysht
Easter	a Páscoa	**pash**-koo-uh

easy	fácil	**fah**-seel
to eat	comer	ko**mehr**
egg	o ovo	**oh**-voo
Elastoplast®	o penso	**payñ**-soo
electric	elétrico(a)	e**le**treekoo(uh)
electric razor	a máquina de barbear	**mak**eenuh duh barbee-**ar**
e-mail	o email	e-**mayl**
embarrassing	embaraçoso(a)	ayñ-barruh-**so**zoo(uh)
embassy	a embaixada	ayñby-**shah**-duh
emergency	a emergência	emehr-**zhayñ**-syuh
emergency exit	a saída de emergência	sah-**ee**duh duh emehr-**zhayñ**-syuh
empty	vazio(a)	vuh-**zee**-oo(uh)
end	o fim	feeñ
engaged	comprometido(a)	koñpro-meh-**tee**-doo(uh)
(phone, toilet, etc.)	ocupado(a)	okoo**pah**-doo(uh)
England	a Inglaterra	eeñ-gluh-**terr**-uh
English	inglês (inglesa)	eeñ**glaysh** (eeñ**glayz**uh)
(language)	o inglês	eeñ**glaysh**
to enjoy oneself	divertir-se	deevehr**teer**-suh
enormous	enorme	eh-**norm**
enough	bastante	bush**tuñt**
that's enough	chega	**sheh**-guh
enquiries	as informações	ush eeñfoormuh-**soyñsh**
enquiry desk	o balcão de informações	bal**kowñ** duh eeñfoormuh-**soyñsh**
to enter	entrar (em)	ayñ-**trar** (ayñ)
enthusiastic	entusiástico(a)	ayñ-too-zee-**ash**-tee-koo(uh)
entrance	a entrada	eñ**trah**-duh
entrance fee	o bilhete de entrada	beel-**yet** duh eñ**trah**-duh
error	o erro	**err**-oo
escalator	a escada rolante	esh**kah**-duh ro**luñt**
estate agent's	a imobiliária	eemoo-bee-lee-**ar**-yuh

euro	o euro	**eoo**-roo
Europe	a Europa	ayoo-**roh**-puh
European	europeu (europeia)	ayoo-roo**peh**-oo (ayoo-roo**peh**-yuh)
eve	a véspera	**vesh**-peruh
evening	a noite; a tardinha	noyt; tuhr**deen**ya
every	cada	**kah**-duh
everyone	toda a gente; todos	**toh**-duh uh zheñt; **toh**-doosh
everything	todas as coisas; tudo	**toh**-dush ush **koy**-zush; **too**doo
everywhere	por todo o lado	poor **toh**-doo oo **lah**-doo
example: ***for example***	por exemplo	poor eh-**zayñ**-ploo
excellent	excelente	esh-se**leñt**
except	exceto	es-**se**too
excess baggage/ luggage	o excesso de bagagem	es-**seh**-soo duh buh-**gah**-zhayñ
to exchange	trocar	troo**kar**
exchange rate	o câmbio	**kuñ**bee-oo
exciting	emocionante	emoh-syo**nuñt**
excuse	a desculpa	dush-**koolp**
exercise (physical)	o exercício	e-zehr-**see**-syoo
exit	a saída	sah-**ee**duh
expenses	as despesas	deesh-**peh**-zush
expensive	caro(a)	**kah**-roo(uh)
expiry date	o prazo de validade	**prah**zoo duh vuhlee**dahd**
to explain	explicar	eesh-plee**kar**
extra	extra	**es**-truh
eye	o olho	**ohl**-yoo

F

facilities	as instalações	eeñstaluh**soyñsh**
to fail	fracassar	fruh-kuh-**sar**
(engine, brakes)	falhar	fal-**yar**
to faint	desmaiar	deesh-my-**ar**
fair (hair)	louro(a)	**loh**-roo(uh)
(just)	justo(a)	**zhoosh**-too(uh)

fake	falso(a)	**fahl**-soo(uh)
to fall	cair	kah-**eer**
he/she has fallen	ele/ela caiu	ayl/**ay**luh kuh-**yoo**
family	a família	fuh-**meel**-yuh
famous	famoso(a)	fuh-**mo**zoo(uh)
far	longe	loñzh
is it far?	é longe?	e loñzh?
how far is it to...?	a que distância fica...?	uh kuh deesh-**tuñss**-yuh **fee**-kuh...?
fare (train, bus, etc.)	o preço (da passagem)	**pray**-soo (duh puh-**sah**-zhayñ)
fast	rápido(a)	**rah**-peedoo(uh)
too fast	rápido(a) demais	**rah**-peedoo(uh) duh-**mysh**
to fasten (seatbelt)	apertar	apehr-**tar**
fat	gordo(a)	**gor**-doo(uh)
father	o pai	py
fault (defect)	o defeito	duh-**fay**-too
favour	o favor	fuh-**vor**
favourite	favorito(a)	fuh-vo**ree**too(uh)
fax	o fax	faks
by fax	por fax	poor faks
to feel	sentir	sayñ-**teer**
I feel sick	tenho náuseas	**ten**-yoo **now**-zee-ush
I don't feel well	sinto-me mal	**seeñ**-too-muh **mahl**
feet	os pés	pesh
female	a mulher	mool-**yehr**
to fetch (to bring)	trazer	truh-**zehr**
(to go and get)	ir buscar	eer boosh-**kar**
fever	a febre	**feb**ruh
few	poucos(as)	**poh**koosh(ush)
a few	alguns (algumas)	al**gooñ** (al**goo**mush)
fiancé(e)	o/a noivo(a)	**noy**voo(uh)
fight	a briga	**bree**guh
to fight	brigar	bree**gar**
to fill	encher	ayñ-**shehr**
fill it up!	encha o depósito!	**ayñ**-shuh oo duh-**poz**eetoo!
to fill in (form)	preencher	prayñ-**shehr**

F

English - Portuguese

fillet	o filete	fee**let**
film (at cinema)	o filme	**feel**muh
to find	achar	a**shar**
fine (to be paid)	a multa	**mool**tuh
to finish	acabar	akuh-**bar**
finished	acabado(a)	akuh-**bah**-doo(uh)
fire	o fogo	**fo**goo
fire alarm	o alarme de incêndios	alarm duh eeñ**sayñ**-dyoosh
fire escape	a saída de emergência	sah-**ee**duh duh emehr-**zhayñ**syuh
fire extinguisher	o extintor	esh-teeñ**tor**
firm (company)	a firma	**feer**muh
first	o/a primeiro(a)	pree**may**-roo(uh)
first aid	os primeiros socorros	pree**may**-roosh soo**korr**oosh
first class	a primeira classe	pree**may**-ruh klass
first name	o nome próprio	nom **prop**ree-oo
fish	o peixe	paysh
to fish	pescar	pesh**kar**
to fit: ***it doesn't fit me***	não me serve	nowñ muh serv
fit	o ataque	uh-**tak**uh
to fix	reparar	repuh-**rar**
fizzy	gasoso(a)	ga**zo**zoo(uh)
flat (apartment)	o apartamento	uh-partuh-**meñ**too
flat	plano(a)	**pluh**-noo(uh)
(battery)	descarregado	desh-karruh-**gah**-doo
flavour	o sabor	suh-**bor**
flight	o voo	**voh**-oo
floor	o chão	showñ
(storey)	o andar	uñ**dar**
ground floor	o rés do chão	resh doo **showñ**
first floor	o primeiro andar	pree**may**-roo uñ**dar**
flower	a flor	flor
flu	a gripe	greep
to fly	voar	voo**ar**
fog	o nevoeiro	nuhvoo**ay**roo
foggy	nevoento	nuhvoo**ayñ**too
food	a comida	ko**mee**duh

food poisoning	a intoxicação alimentar	eeñtokseekuh-**sowñ** aleemeñ**tar**
foot	o pé	pe
on foot	a pé	uh pe
football	o futebol	foot**bol**
for	para	**pa**ruh
for me	para mim	**pa**ruh meeñ
forbidden	proibido(a)	proee-**bee**doo(uh)
forecast	a previsão	previsão
weather forecast	a previsão do tempo	prevee**zowñ** doo t**ayñ**poo
foreign	estrangeiro(a)	eesh-truñ-**zhay**-roo(uh)
foreigner	o/a estrangeiro(a)	eesh-truñ-**zhay**-roo(uh)
forever	para sempre	**pa**ruh **sayñ**pruh
to forget	esquecer-se de	eesh-kuh-**ser**-suh duh
fork (for eating)	o garfo	**gar**foo
(in road)	a bifurcação	bee-foorkuh-**sowñ**
form (document)	o formulário	formoo-**lar**yoo
fracture	a fratura	fru**too**ruh
fragile	frágil	**frah**-zheel
free (not occupied)	livre	**lee**-vree
(costing nothing)	grátis	**grah**-teesh
freezer	o congelador	koñzhuh-luh-**dor**
frequent	frequente	fruh-**kweñt**
fresh	fresco(a)	**fresh**-koo(uh)
Friday	a sexta-feira	**sesh**tuh-**fay**ruh
fried	frito(a)	**free**too(uh)
friend	o/a amigo(a)	uh-**mee**goo(uh)
friendly	simpático(a)	seeñ**pah**-teekoo(uh)
from	de	duh
from England	da Inglaterra	duh eeñ-gluh-**terr**-uh
front	a frente	freñt
in front of	em frente de	ayñ freñt duh
fruit	a fruta	**froo**tuh
to fry	fritar	free**tar**
fuel (petrol)	a gasolina	gazoo**lee**-nuh
full	cheio(a)	**shay**oo(uh)

full board	a pensão completa	payñ-**sowñ** koñ**pleh**-tuh
fun	a diversão	deevehr-**sowñ**
funny	engraçado(a)	eeñgruh-**sah**doo(uh)
(strange)	estranho(a)	ees**trun**-yoo(uh)
furnished	mobilado(a)	moobee**lah**-doo
furniture	a mobília	moo**beel**-yuh

G

gallery (art)	a galeria de arte	galeh-**ree**-uh duh art
game	o jogo	**zhoh**-goo
garage (private)	a garagem	guh-**rah**-zheñ
(for repairs)	a oficina (de reparações)	oofee-**see**nuh (duh reparuh-**soyñsh**)
(for petrol)	a estação de serviço	shta**sowñ** duh ser**vee**soo
garden	o jardim	zhar**deeñ**
gas	o gás	gahs
generous	generoso(a)	zhene**ro**zoo(uh)
gents' (toilet)	Homens	**om**ayñsh
genuine (leather, antique etc.)	autêntico(a)	ow**tayñ**teekoo(uh)
to get (to obtain)	obter	ob**tehr**
(to receive)	receber	ruh-seh-**behr**
(to fetch)	ir buscar	eer boosh**kar**
to get in (vehicle)	entrar em	ayñ-**trar** ayñ
to get into	entrar em	ayñ-**trar** ayñ
to get off	descer de	desh-**sehr** duh
to get on (vehicle)	entrar em	ayñ-**trar** ayñ
gift	o presente; a prenda	pruh-**zeñt**; uh **prayn**-duh
gift shop	a loja de lembranças	**lo**zhuh duh layñ-**bruñ**-sush
girl	a rapariga	ruh-pa**ree**guh
girlfriend	a namorada	namoo**rah**-duh
to give	dar	dar
to give back	devolver	duh-vol**vehr**
glass (substance)	o vidro; o cristal	**vee**droo; kreesh-**tahl**
(to drink out of)	o copo	**kop**oo
glasses	os óculos	oosh **oh**-kooloosh

to go	ir	eer
I'm going to...	vou para...	voh **pa**ruh...
we're going to...	vamos para...	**vuh**-moosh **pa**ruh...
to go back	voltar	vol**tar**
to go down	descer	desh-**sehr**
to go in	entrar (em)	ayñ-**trar** (ayñ)
to go out	sair	sah-**eer**
good	bom (boa)	boñ (**boh**-uh)
very good	muito bom	**mweeñ**to boñ
gram	o grama	**gruh**-muh
grandchild	o/a neto(a)	**neh**-too(uh)
grandparents	os avós	oosh uh-**vosh**
grapes	as uvas	ush **oo**vush
great (big)	grande	gruñd
(wonderful)	ótimo(a)	**o**tee-moo(uh)
Great Britain	a Grã-Bretanha	grañ-bruh-**tun**-yuh
green	verde	verd
greengrocer's	a frutaria	frootuh-**ree**-uh
grocer's	a mercearia	mehrsee-uh-**ree**-uh
ground (earth)	a terra	**terr**-uh
(floor)	o chão	**showñ**
ground floor	o rés do chão	resh-doo-**showñ**
on the ground floor...	no rés do chão...	noo resh-doo-**showñ**...
group	o grupo	**groo**poo
guarantee	a garantia	guh-ruñ**tee**-uh
guest	o/a convidado(a)	koñvee**dah**-doo(uh)
(in hotel)	o/a hóspede	**osh**-peeduh
guesthouse	a pensão	payñ-**sowñ**
guide	o/a guia	**ghee**-uh
guidebook	o guia	**ghee**-uh
guided tour	a excursão guiada	eeshkoor**sowñ** ghee-**ah**-duh

H

hair	o cabelo	kuh-**bay**-loo
hairdresser	o/a cabeleireiro(a)	kuh-bay-lay-**ray**-roo(uh)
half	a metade	meh-**tahd**

a half bottle of	meia garrafa de	**may**uh ga**rrah**-fuh duh
half an hour	meia hora	**may**uh **or**uh
half board	a meia pensão	**may**uh payñ-**sowñ**
half fare	meio-bilhete	**may**oo beel-**yet**
half-price	pela metade do preço	peluh meh-**tahd** doo **pray**-soo
ham (boiled)	fiambre	fee-**uñ**-bruh
(smoked)	presunto	pruh-**zoon**too
hamburger	o hambúrguer	uñ**boor**gehr
hand	a mão	mowñ
handbag	a bolsa	**bol**suh
handicapped (person)	o/a deficiente	duh-feess-**yeñt**
hand luggage	a bagagem de mão	buh-**gah**-zhayñ duh mowñ
hand-made	feito(a) à mão	**fay**too(uh) a mowñ
handsome	bonito(a)	boo**nee**too(uh)
to hang up (phone)	desligar	deesh-lee**gar**
to happen	acontecer	uh-koñte**sehr**
what happened?	o que aconteceu?	oo kuh uh-koñte**say**oo?
happy	feliz	fuh-**leesh**
hard	duro(a)	**doo**-roo(uh)
(difficult)	difícil	dee**fee**seel
to have	ter	tehr
I (don't) have...	eu (não) tenho...	**ay**-oo (nowñ) **ten**-yoo...
we (don't) have...	nós (não) temos...	nosh (nowñ) **tay**moosh...
do you have...?	tem...?	tayñ...?
to have to	ter de	tehr duh
hay fever	a febre dos fenos	**feb**ruh doosh **feh**-noosh
he	ele	ayl
headache	a dor de cabeça	dor duh kuh-**beh**-suh
I have a headache	dói-me a cabeça	**doy**-muh uh kuh-**beh**-suh
health	a saúde	sah-**ood**
healthy	saudável	sow**dah**-vel

English	Portuguese	Pronunciation
to hear	ouvir	oh-**veer**
heart	o coração	kooruh-**sowñ**
to heat up	aquecer	akuh-**sehr**
heavy	pesado(a)	peh-**zah**-doo(uh)
height	a altura	al**too**ruh
hello	olá	oh-**lah**
(on phone)	está?	shta?
help	a ajuda	uh-**zhoo**duh
help!	socorro!	soo**korr**oo!
to help	ajudar	azhoo**dar**
can you help me?	pode-me ajudar?	**pod**-muh azhoo**dar?**
here	aqui	uh-**kee**
hi!	olá!	oh-**lah**!
to hide (something)	esconder	eeshkoñ**dehr**
(oneself)	esconder-se	eeshkoñ**dehr**-suh
high (price, speed, building)	alto(a)	**ahl**too(uh)
(number)	grande	gruñd
him (direct object)	o	oo
(indirect object)	lhe	lyuh
(after preposition)	ele	ayl
hire	o aluguer	aloo**gehr**
car hire	o aluguer de carros	aloo**gehr** duh **karr**oosh
to hire	alugar	aloo**gar**
hobby	o passatempo	passuh-**tayñ**-poo
to hold (to contain)	conter	koñ**tehr**
holiday	as férias	**fehr**-yush
(public holiday)	o feriado	fuh-ree-**ah**-doo
on holiday	de férias	duh **fehr**-yush
home	a casa	**kah**-zuh
at home	em casa	ayñ **kah**-zuh
to go home	voltar para casa	vol**tar pa**ruh **kah**-zuh
honeymoon	a lua de mel	**loo**-uh duh mel
to hope	esperar	eesh-peh-**rar**
I hope so/not	espero que sim/não	eesh-**peh**-roo kuh seeñ/nowñ
hospital	o hospital	oshpee**tahl**
hot	quente	keñt
I'm hot	tenho calor	**ten**-yoo ka**lor**

it's hot	está quente	shta keñt
it's hot (weather)	faz/está calor	fash/shta ka**lor**
hotel	o hotel	oh-**tel**
hour	a hora	**or**uh
half an hour	meia hora	**may**uh **or**uh
1 hour	uma hora	**oo**muh **or**uh
2 hours	duas horas	**doo**-ush **or**uz
house	a casa	**kah**-zuh
how	como	**koh**-moo
how much?	quanto(a)?	**kwuñ**too(uh)?
how many?	quantos(as)?	**kwuñ**toosh(ush)?
how are you?	como está?	**koh**-moo shta?
hundred	cem	sayñ
hungry: *I am hungry*	tenho fome	**ten**-yoo fom
hurry: *I'm in a hurry*	tenho pressa	**ten**-yoo **preh**-suh
to hurt	doer	doo-**ehr**
that hurts	isso dói	**e**-soo **doy**
husband	o marido	muh**ree**doo

I

I	eu	**ay**-oo
ice	o gelo	**zhay**-loo
ice cream	o gelado	zhuh-**lah**-doo
ice lolly	o gelado	zhuh-**lah**-doo
identity card	o bilhete de identidade	beel-**yet** duh eedeñtee**dahd**
if	se	suh
ill	doente	doo-**eñt**
I'm ill	estou doente	shto doo-**eñt**
illness	a doença	doo-**ayñ**suh
immediately	imediatamente	eemuh-dee-ah-tuh-**meñt**
important	importante	eeñpor**tuñt**
impossible	impossível	eeñpoo-**see**-vel
to improve	melhorar	mel-yo**rar**
in	em	ayñ
(within)	dentro de	**deñ**troo duh

in 10 minutes	dentro de dez minutos	**deñ**troo duh desh mee**noo**tosh
in London	em Londres	ayñ **loñ**drush
in front of	em frente de	ayñ freñt duh
included	incluído(a)	eeñkloo-**ee**doo(uh)
to increase	aumentar	owmeñ**tar**
indigestion	a indigestão	eeñdee-zhesh-**towñ**
infection	a infeção	eeñfe-**sowñ**
information	a informação	eeñfoormuh-**sowñ**
to injure	lesionar	leh-zyo**nar**
injured	ferido(a)	fuh-**ree**doo(uh)
inquiries	as informações	eeñfoormuh-**soyñsh**
insect	o inseto	eeñ**seh**-too
inside	dentro	**deñ**troo
instead of	em vez de	ayñ vesh duh
insurance	o seguro	se**goo**roo
insurance certificate	a apólice de seguro	uh-**pol**eesee duh se**goo**roo
insured: ***to be insured***	estar no seguro	esh-**tar** noo se**goo**roo
intelligent	inteligente	eeñteh-lee-**zheñt**
to intend to	tencionar	tayñ-syo**nar**
interesting	interessante	eeñteh-reh-**ssuñt**
internet	a internet	eeñter**net**
international	internacional	eeñternasyo**nahl**
into	em; a; para	ayñ; uh; **pa**ruh
into the centre	ao centro	ow **señ**troo
invitation	o convite	koñ**veet**
to invite	convidar	koñvee**dar**
Ireland	a Irlanda	eer**luñ**duh
Irish	irlandês (irlandesa)	eerluñ**daysh** (eerluñ**day**-zuh)
iron (metal)	o ferro	**ferr**-oo
(for clothes)	o ferro de engomar	**ferr**-oo duh ayñgo**mar**
island	a ilha	**eel**-yuh
to itch	fazer comichão	fa**zehr** komee**showñ**
it itches	faz comichão	fash komee**showñ**

J

jacket	o casaco	kuh-**zah**-koo
jam	a compota	koñ**po**tuh
jammed (stuck)	bloqueado(a)	bloh-kee-**ah**-doo(uh)
jar	o frasco	**frahsh**koo
jealous	ciumento(a)	syoo**meñ**too(uh)
jeans	as jeans	zheeñsh
jewel	a joia	**zhoy**-uh
jewellery	a joalharia	zhwal-yuh-**ree**-uh
job	o emprego	ayñ-**preh**-goo
to join (club)	associar-se a	assossee**ar**-suh
to join in	participar	partee-see**par**
to joke	brincar	breeñ**kar**
journalist	o/a jornalista	zhorna**leesh**tuh
journey	a viagem	vee-**ah**-zhayñ
juice	o sumo	**soo**moo
to jump	saltar	sal**tar**
junction	o cruzamento	kroozuh-**meñ**too
just: ***just two***	apenas dois	uh-**peh**-nush doysh
I've just arrived	acabo de chegar	uh-**kah**-boo duh shuh-**gar**

K

to keep	guardar	gwar**dar**
(retain)	ficar com	fee**kar** koñ
keep the change!	fique com o troco!	feek koñ oo **tro**koo!
key	a chave	shahv
to kill	matar	muh-**tar**
kilo	o quilo	**kee**loo
kilometre	o quilómetro	kee**lom**etroo
kind (person)	amável	uh-**mah**-vel
kind (sort)	a espécie	eesh**pess**ee-uh
kiosk	o quiosque	**kee**-oshk
kiss	o beijo	**bay**-zhoo
to kiss	beijar	bay-**zhar**
kitchen	a cozinha	koo**zeen**-yuh
to knock (on door)	bater	buh-**tehr**
to know (have knowledge of)	saber	suh-**behr**

(person, place)	conhecer	koon-yeh-**sehr**
I don't know	não sei	nowñ **say**
to know how to swim	saber nadar	suh-**behr** nuh-**dar**

L

lady	a senhora	sun-**yo**ruh
lager	a cerveja	ser**vay**-zhuh
bottled lager	a cerveja de garrafa	ser**vay**-zhuh duh ga**rrah**-fuh
draught lager	a imperial	eeñpehr-**yahl**
lamb	o cordeiro	koor-**day**-roo
to land	aterrar	ate**rrar**
language	a língua	**leeñ**gwuh
large	grande	gruñd
last	último(a)	**ool**teemoo(uh)
last night	ontem à noite	**oñ**-tayñ a noyt
last week	a semana passada	suh-**mah**-nuh puh-**sah**-duh
last year	o ano passado	**ah**-noo puh-**sah**-doo
the last time	a última vez	**ool**teemuh vesh
late	tarde	tard
the train is late	o comboio está atrasado	koñ**boy**oo shta atruh-**zah**-doo
sorry we are late	desculpe o atraso	dush**koolp** oo uh-**trah**-zoo
later	mais tarde	mysh tard
to laugh	rir	reer
lavatory	a casa de banho	**kah**-zuh duh **buhn**yoo
law	a lei	lay
to learn	aprender	aprayñ-**dehr**
least: ***at least***	pelo menos	**peh**-loo **meh**-noosh
leather	o couro	**koh**-roo
to leave (leave behind)	deixar	day-**shar**
(train, bus etc.)	partir	par**teer**
when does it leave?	a que horas parte?	a kee **or**uz part?
left: ***on/to the left***	à esquerda	a **shkehr**-duh

left luggage (office)	o depósito de bagagens	duh-**poz**eetoo duh buh-**gah**-zhayñs
leg	a perna	**pehr**-nuh
lemonade	a limonada	leemo**nah**-duh
to lend	emprestar	aympresh-**tar**
length	o comprimento	koñpree**meñ**too
lenses (contact lenses)	as lentes de contacto	ush leñtsh duh koñ**tak**too
less	menos	**meh**-noosh
less than	menos do que	**meh**-noosh doo kuh
let (allow)	deixar	day-**shar**
(lease)	alugar	aloo**gar**
letter	a carta	**kar**tuh
(of alphabet)	a letra	**let**ruh
licence	a licença	lee-**sayñ**-suh
(driving)	a carta de condução	**kar**tuh duh koñdoo**sowñ**
lie (untruth)	a mentira	meñ**tee**ruh
life	a vida	**vee**-duh
lift (elevator)	o elevador	eeluh-vuh-**dor**
(in car)	a boleia	boo-**lay**-uh
light	a luz	loosh
light (not heavy)	leve	lev
(colour)	claro(a)	**klah**-roo(uh)
like	como	**koh**-moo
it's like this	é assim	e uh-**seeñ**
to like	gostar de	goosh**tar** duh
I (don't) like coffee	(não) gosto de café	(nowñ) **gosh**too duh kuh-**fe**
I'd like to...	gostava de...	goosh**tah**-vuh duh...
we'd like to...	gostávamos de...	goosh**tah**-vuh-moosh duh...
line (row, queue)	a fila	**fee**luh
(phone)	a linha	**leen**-yuh
list	a lista	**leesh**tuh
to listen to	ouvir	oh-**veer**
litre	o litro	**lee**troo
litter (rubbish)	o lixo	**lee**shoo
little	pequeno(a)	puh-**kay**noo(uh)
a little...	um pouco de...	ooñ **poh**koo duh...

English	Portuguese	Pronunciation
to live	viver; morar	vee**vehr**; moo**rar**
local	local	lo**kahl**
to lock	fechar à chave	fuh-**shar** a shahv
locker (luggage)	o depósito de bagagem	duh-**poz**eetoo duh buh-**gah**-zhayñ
London	Londres	**loñ**drush
in London	em Londres	ayñ **loñ**drush
to London	a Londres	a **loñ**drush
long	comprido(a); longo(a)	koñ**pree**doo(uh); **loñ**goo(uh)
for a long time	durante muito tempo	doo**ruñt mweeñ**to tayñ-poo
to look after	cuidar de	kwee-**dar** duh
to look at	olhar	ol-**yar**
to look for	procurar	prokoo**rar**
to lose	perder	pehr-**dehr**
lost	perdido(a)	pehr-**dee**doo(uh)
I have lost my wallet	perdi a minha carteira	pehr-**dee** uh **meen**-yuh kar-**tay**-ruh
I am lost	estou perdido(a)	shto pehr-**dee**doo(uh)
lost property office	a secção de perdidos e achados	sek**sowñ** duh per**dee**-doosh ee uh-**shah**-doosh
lot: ***a lot*** (much)	muito(a)	**mweeñ**too(uh)
(many)	muitos(as)	**mweeñ**toosh(ush)
loud (noisy)	ruidoso(a)	rwee-**do**zoo(uh)
(volume)	alto(a)	**ahl**too(uh)
lounge (in hotel, house)	a sala de estar	**sah**-luh duh esh-**tar**
(in airport)	a sala	**sah**-luh
to love	amar	ah-**mar**
I love swimming	adoro nadar	uh-**dor**oo nuh-**dar**
lovely	encantador(a)	eeñkuñtuh-**dor**(uh)
low	baixo(a)	**by**shoo(uh)
lucky: ***to be lucky***	ter sorte	tehr sort
luggage	a bagagem	buh-**gah**-zhayñ
lunch	o almoço	al**moh**-soo
luxury	o luxo	**loo**-shoo

M

English	Portuguese	Pronunciation
machine	a máquina	**mak**eenuh
madam	a senhora	sun-**yo**ruh
magazine	a revista	ru**veesh**-tuh
maid	a empregada	eeñpre**gah**-duh
mail	o correio	koo**rray**oo
by mail	pelo correio	**peh**-loo koo**rray**oo
main	principal	preeñsee**pahl**
main course (of meal)	o prato principal	**prah**-too preeñsee**pahl**
main road	a estrada principal	**shtrah**-duh preeñsee**pahl**
to make (generally)	fazer	fa**zehr**
(meal)	preparar	preh-pa**rar**
make-up	a maquilhagem	muh-keel-**yah**-zhayñ
male	masculino(a)	mash-koo**lee**noo(uh)
man	o homem	**om**ayñ
to manage (cope)	arranjar-se	arruñ**zhar** -suh
manager	o/a gerente	zhe**reñt**
many	muitos(as)	**mweeñ**toosh(ush)
map	o mapa	**mah**-puh
market	o mercado	mer**kah**-doo
where is the market?	onde fica o mercado?	**oñ**duh **fee**kuh oo mer**kah**-doo?
when is the market?	quando há mercado?	**kwuñ**doo a mer**kah**-doo?
married	casado(a)	kuh-**zah**-doo(uh)
I'm married	sou casado(a)	soh kuh-**zah**-doo(uh)
are you married?	é casado(a)?	e kuh-**zah**-doo(uh)?
to get married	casar(-se)	kuh-**zar**(-suh)
material	o material	matehr-**yahl**
(cloth)	o tecido	teh-**see**doo
to matter: ***it doesn't matter***	não tem importância	nowñ tayñ eeñpoor**tuñss**-yuh
maximum	o máximo	**mah**-seemoo
meal	a refeição	ruhfay**sowñ**
to mean	significar	seeg-neefee**kar**
what does this mean?	o que quer dizer isto?	oh kee kehr dee**zehr** **eesh**too?
to measure	medir	meh-**deer**

meat	a carne	karn
I don't eat meat	não como carne	nowñ **koh**-moo karn
medicine	o medicamento	medeekuh-**meñ**too
medium	médio(a)	**med**-yoo(uh)
medium rare (meat)	meio-passado(a)	**may**oo puh-**sah**-doo(uh)
to meet (by chance)	encontrar	ayñkoñ**trar**
(by arrangement)	encontrar-se com	ayñkoñ**trar**-suh koñ
pleased to meet you	prazer em conhecê-lo(a)	pruh-**zehr** ayñ koon-ye-**say**-loo(uh)
memory	a memória	meh-**mor**-yuh
(thing remembered)	a lembrança	layñ-**bruñ**-suh
memory card (for digital camera)	o cartão memória	kar**towñ** meh-**mor**-yuh
men	os homens	**oh**mayñsh
to mend	arranjar; consertar	arruñ**zhar**; koñsehr**tar**
menu	a ementa	ee**meñ**tuh
set menu	a ementa fixa	ee**meñ**tuh **feek**suh
à la carte menu	a ementa a la carte	ee**meñ**tuh a la kart
message	a mensagem	meñ**sah**-zhayñ
metre	o metro	**me**troo
midday	o meio-dia	**may**oo-**dee**-uh
at midday	ao meio-dia	ow **may**oo-**dee**-uh
middle	o meio	**may**oo
midnight	a meia-noite	**may**uh-noyt
at midnight	à meia-noite	a **may**uh-noyt
mile	a milha	**meel**-yuh
milk	o leite	layt
full-cream milk	o leite gordo	layt **gor**-doo
semi-skimmed milk	o leite meio-gordo	layt **may**oo **gor**-doo
skimmed milk	o leite magro	layt **mah**groo
with milk	com leite	koñ layt
without milk	sem leite	sayñ layt
million	o milhão	meel-**yowñ**
to mind (take care of)	ocupar-se de	okoo**par**-suh duh
do you mind if...?	importa-se?	eeñ**por**tuh-suh?
I don't mind	não me importo	nowñ muh eeñ**por**too

M

English - Portuguese

minimum	o mínimo	**mee**neemoo
minute	o minuto	mee**noo**too
Miss...	Menina...	muh-**nee**nuh...
to miss (plane, train, etc.)	perder	pehr-**dehr**
missing (lost)	perdido(a)	pehr-**dee**doo(uh)
mistake	o erro	**err**-oo
to mix	misturar	meestu**rar**
mobile phone	o telemóvel	tuh-luh-**mo**vel
modern	moderno(a)	moo**dehr**-noo(uh)
moment: ***just a moment***	um momento	ooñ mo**meñ**too
Monday	a segunda-feira	suh**goon**-duh **fay**ruh
money	o dinheiro	deen-**yay**-roo
I've no money	não tenho dinheiro	nowñ **ten**-yoo deen-**yay**-roo
month	o mês	maysh
this month	este mês	aysht maysh
last month	o mês passado	maysh puh-**sah**-doo
next month	o mês que vem	maysh kee vayñ
more	mais	mysh
more than 3	mais de três	mysh duh traysh
more bread	mais pão	mysh powñ
more wine	mais vinho	mysh **veen**-yoo
morning	a manhã	mun-**yañ**
in the morning	de manhã	duh mun-**yañ**
this morning	esta manhã	**esh**tuh mun-**yañ**
tomorrow morning	amanhã de manhã	amun-**yañ** duh mun-**yañ**
most: ***most of***	a maioria de	uh my-o-**ree**-uh duh
mother	a mãe	**mah**-ee
motor	o motor	mo**tor**
motorbike	a moto	**mo**to
motorway	a auto estrada	owtoo **shtrah**-duh
mouth	a boca	**bo**kuh
to move	mexer; mover	me**shehr**; mo**vehr**
Mr	o Senhor	sun-**yor**
Mrs	a Senhora	sun-**yo**ruh
Ms	a Senhora	sun-**yo**ruh
much	muito(a)	**mweeñ**too

too much	demais	duh-mysh
mugging	o assalto	uh-**sahl**too
muscle	o músculo	**moosh**-kooloo
museum	o museu	moo-**zay**-oo
music	a música	**moo**zeekuh
must (to have to)	dever	de**vehr**
I must	devo	**deh**-voo
we must	devemos	duh-**veh**-moosh
I mustn't	não devo	nowñ **deh**-voo
we mustn't	não devemos	nowñ duh-**veh**-moosh
my	meu (minha)	**may**oo (**meen**-yuh)

N

name	o nome	nom
narrow	estreito(a)	ees**tray**too(uh)
national	nacional	nasyo**nahl**
nationality	a nacionalidade	nasyo-nalee**dahd**
natural	natural	natoo**rahl**
nature	a natureza	natoo-**reh**-zuh
near	perto	**pehr**too
near the bank	perto do banco	**pehr**too doo **buñ**koo
is it near?	fica perto?	feekuh **pehr**too?
necessary	necessário(a)	nussuh-**sar**-yoo(uh)
to need	precisar de	presee**zar** duh
I need...	preciso de	pre-**see**zoo duh
we need...	precisamos de	presee**zah**-moosh duh
I need to go	tenho que ir	**ten**-yoo kuh eer
never	nunca	**noon**kuh
I never drink wine	nunca bebo vinho	**noon**-kuh **beh**-boo **veen**yoo
new	novo(a)	**noh**-voo(uh)
news	a notícia	no**tee**seeuh
(on television)	o noticiário; o telejornal	noteesee-**ar**yoo; telezhoor**nahl**
newspaper	o jornal	zhoor**nahl**
New Year	o Ano Novo	**ah**-noo **noh**-voo
New Year's Eve	a véspera de Ano Novo	**vesh**-peruh duh **ah**-noo **noh**-voo

New Zealand	a Nova Zelândia	**noh**-vuh zeh-**luñ**dyuh
next	próximo(a)	**pross**eemoo(uh)
next to	ao lado de	ow **lah**-doo duh
next week	a semana que vem	suh-**mah**-nuh kuh vayñ
the next bus	o próximo autocarro	**pross**eemoo owtoo-**karr**oo
the next stop	a próxima paragem	**pross**eemuh pa**rah**-zhayñ
nice (person)	simpático(a)	seeñ-**pah**-teekoo(uh)
(place)	bonito(a)	boo**nee**too(uh)
night	a noite	noyt
at night	à noite	a noyt
last night	ontem à noite	**oñ**-tayñ a noyt
per night	por noite	poor noyt
tomorrow night	amanhã à noite	amun-**yañ** a noyt
no	não	nowñ
no entry	entrada proibida	eñ**trah**-duh pro-ee**bee**duh
no smoking	proibido fumar	proee-**bee**doo foo**mar**
no thanks	não, obrigado(a)	nowñ, oh-bree**gah**-doo(uh)
nobody	ninguém	neeñ**gayñ**
noise	o barulho	ba**rool**-yoo
noisy	barulhento(a)	barool-**yeñ**too(uh)
non-alcoholic	sem álcool	seyñ al**kol**
none	nenhum(a)	nayn-**ooñ** (nayn-**oo**muh)
there's none left	não sobrou nada	nowñ so**broh nah**-duh
non-smoker	o/a não-fumador(a)	nowñ foomuh-**dor**(uh)
non-smoking	não-fumador(a)	nowñ foomuh-**dor**(uh)
north	o norte	nort
Northern Ireland	a Irlanda do Norte	eer**luñ**duh doo nort
not	não	nowñ
note (letter)	a nota	**no**tuh
nothing	nada	**nah**-duh

English	Portuguese	Pronunciation
nothing else	mais nada	mysh **nah**-duh
notice	o aviso	uh-**vee**soo
now	agora	uh-**gor**uh
nowhere (be)	em nenhum lugar	ayñ nayn-**yooñ** loo**gar**
(go)	a lugar nenhum	uh loo**gar** nayn-**yooñ**
number	o número	**noo**meroo

O

English	Portuguese	Pronunciation
to obtain	obter	ob**tehr**
occasionally	às vezes	ush **veh**-zush
of	de	duh
a bottle of water	uma garrafa de água	**oo**muh ga**rrah**-fuh duh **ahg**-wuh
a glass of wine	um copo de vinho	ooñ **kop**oo duh **veen**-yoo
made of...	feito(a) de...	**fay**-too(uh) duh...
off (radio, engine, etc.)	desligado(a)	deesh-lee**gah**-doo(uh)
(milk, food, etc.)	estragado(a)	eestruh-**gah**-doo(uh)
this meat is off	esta carne está estragada	**esh**tuh karn shta eestruh-**gah**-duh
office	o escritório	eeshkree-**tor**yoo
often	muitas vezes	**mweeñ**tush **veh**-zush
how often?	quantas vezes?	**kwuñ**tush **veh**-zush?
OK	está bem	shta bayñ
old	velho(a)	**vel**-yoo(uh)
how old are you?	quantos anos tem?	**kwuñ**toosh **ah**-noosh tayñ?
I'm ... years old	tenho ... anos	**ten**-yoo ... **ah**-noosh
on (light, TV)	aceso(a)	uh-**seh**-zoo(uh)
(engine)	a trabalhar	uh trabal-**yar**
on	em	ayñ
on the table	na mesa	nuh **may**-zuh
on time	a horas	uh **or**uz
once	uma vez	**oo**muh vesh
at once	imediatamente	eemeh-dee-ah-tuh-**meñt**
only	somente	so**meñt**

adj	único(a)	**oo**neekoo(uh)
open adj	aberto(a)	uh-**behr**-too
to open	abrir	uh-**breer**
or	ou	oh
tea or coffee?	chá ou café?	shah oh kuh-**fe**?
orange adj	cor de laranja	kor duh la**ruñ**zhuh
orange (fruit)	a laranja	la**ruñ**zhuh
orange juice	o sumo de laranja	s**oo**moo duh la**ruñ**zhuh
order: ***out of order***	fora de serviço; avariado(a)	**for**-uh duh ser**vee**soo; avaree-**ah**-doo(uh)
to order (in restaurant)	pedir	ped**eer**
to organize	organizar	orguh-nee**zar**
other: ***the other one***	o/a outro(a)	**oh**-troo(truh)
have you any others?	tem outros(as)?	tayñ **oh**-troosh(trush)?
our	nosso(a)	**noss**oo(uh)
out	fora	**for**-uh
he's gone out	ele saiu	ayl sah-**yoo**
he's out	não está	nowñ shta
outside: ***it's outside***	está lá fora	shta lah **for**-uh
over (on top of)	sobre	**sob**ruh
to be overbooked	ter mais reservas que lugares	tehr mysh ruh-**zehr**vush kuh loo**gah**-rush
to overcharge	cobrar a mais	ko**brar** a mysh
overdone (food)	cozido demais	koo**zee**doo duh-mysh
to owe	dever	de**vehr**
you owe me...	deve-me...	**dev**-muh...
I owe you...	devo-lhe...	**deh**-voo-lyuh...

P

package	o embrulho	eeñ**brool**-yoo
package tour	o pacote turístico	pakot too**reesh**teekoo
paid	pago(a)	**pah**-goo(uh)
pain	a dor	dor

painful	doloroso(a)	dolo**ro**zoo(uh)
painkiller	o analgésico	anal**zheh**-zeekoo
pair	o par	par
paper	o papel	puh-**pel**
(newspaper)	o jornal	zhoor**nahl**
paracetamol	o paracetamol	paruh-seetuh-**mol**
parcel	a encomenda	eeñkoo**meñ**duh
pardon	desculpe?	dush**koolp**?
I beg your pardon!	peço desculpa	**peh**soo dush**kool**puh
parents	os pais	oosh pysh
to park	estacionar	eesh-tassyoo**nar**
parking ticket	a multa	**mool**tuh
part	a parte	part
partner (business)	o/a sócio(a)	**soh**-seeoo(uh)
(friend)	o/a companheiro(a)	koñpun-**yay**-roo(uh)
party (celebration)	a festa	**fesh**-tuh
(political)	o partido	par**tee**doo
passenger	o/a passageiro(a)	passuh-**zhay**-roo(uh)
passport	o passaporte	passuh-**port**
pasta	a massa	**mass**uh
pastry (dough)	a massa	**mass**uh
(cake)	o bolo	**boh**loo
patient (adj)	paciente	passee-**eñt**
to pay	pagar	puh-**gar**
I'd like to pay	quero pagar	**kay**roo puh-**gar**
where do I pay?	onde é que se paga?	**oñ**duh e kuh suh **pah**-guh?
payment	o pagamento	paguh-**meñ**too
payphone	o telefone público	tuh-luh-**fo**nee **poob**leekoo
peanut allergy	a alergia a amendoins	alehr-**zhee**-uh a ameñdoo**eeñsh**
pear	a pera	**pay**-ruh
pedestrian crossing	a passadeira para peões	passuh-**day**-ruh **par**uh peh-**oyñsh**
pen	a caneta	kuh-**neh**-tuh
pencil	o lápis	**lah**-peesh
pension	a pensão	payñ-**sowñ**
pensioner	o/a reformado(a)	refoor**mah**-doo(uh)
people	as pessoas	ush puh-**so**-ush

pepper (spice)	a pimenta	pee**meñ**tuh
(vegetable)	o pimento	pee**meñ**too
per	por	poor
per hour	por hora	poor **or**uh
perfect	perfeito(a)	pehr-**fay**-too(uh)
perhaps	talvez	tal**vesh**
person	a pessoa	puh-**so**-uh
per person	por pessoa	poor puh-**so**-uh
petrol	a gasolina	gazoo**lee**nuh
pharmacy	a farmácia	far**mass**-yuh
phone	o telefone	tuh-luh-**fo**nee
mobile phone	o telemóvel	tuh-luh-**mo**vel
to phone	telefonar	tuh-luh-fo**nar**
phone box	a cabine telefónica	kuh-**been**-uh tuh-luh-**fo**neekuh
photocopy	a fotocópia	foto**koh**-pyuh
photograph	a fotografia	footoogruh-**fee**-uh
to take a photograph	tirar uma fotografia	tee**rar oo**muh footoogruh-**fee**-uh
phrasebook	o guia de conversação	**ghee**-uh duh koñversuh-**sowñ**
to pick (fruit, flowers)	colher	kohl-**yer**
(to choose)	escolher	eeshkohl-**yer**
pickpocket	o/a carteirista	kartay-**reesh**-tuh
picture (painting)	o quadro	**kwad**roo
(photo)	a foto	**fot**oo
piece	o bocado; o pedaço	boo**kah**-doo; puh-**dah**-ssoo
pig	o porco	**por**koo
pill	o comprimido	koñpree**mee**doo
to be on the pill	tomar a pílula	too**mar** uh **pee**looluh
pilot	o/a piloto(a)	pee**loh**too(uh)
pink	cor de rosa	kor duh **roh**-zuh
pint	= approx. 0.5 litre	
a pint of beer	uma caneca de cerveja	**oo**muh ka**neh**kuh duh ser**vay**-zhuh
pizza	a pizza	**pee**zuh
place	o lugar	loo**gar**
plan	o plano	**pluhn**-oo

English	Portuguese	Pronunciation
to plan	planear	pluh-nee-**ar**
plane	o avião	av-**yowñ**
plaster (sticking)	o adesivo	adeh-**zee**voo
(for broken limb)	o gesso	**zhess**oo
plastic	o plástico	**plash**-teekoo
platform (railway)	o cais	kysh
play (at theatre)	a peça	**peh**-suh
to play (sport)	jogar	zhoo**gar**
(musical instrument)	tocar	too**kar**
(general play)	brincar	breeñ**kar**
pleasant	agradável	agruh-**dah**-vel
please	por favor; faz favor	poor fuh-**vor**; fash fuh-**vor**
pleased: ***pleased to meet you***	prazer em conhecê-lo(a)	pruh-**zehr** ayñ koon-ye-**say**-loo(uh)
plenty: ***plenty of*** (much)	muito(a)	**mweeñ**too(uh)
(many)	muitos(as)	**mweeñ**toosh(ush)
p.m. (afternoon/ evening)	de tarde	duh tard
(night)	de noite	duh noyt
police (force)	a polícia	poo**lee**-syuh
police station	a esquadra	eesh-**kwah**-druh
pool	a piscina	peesh-**see**nuh
poor	pobre	**po**bree
pork	a carne de porco	karn duh **por**koo
port (wine)	o vinho do porto	**veen**-yoo doo **por**too
(seaport)	o porto	**por**too
portion	a dose	**doh**-suh
Portugal	Portugal	poortoo**gahl**
Portuguese	português (portuguesa)	poortoo-**gaysh** (poortoo-**gay**-zuh)
(language)	o português	poortoo-**gaysh**
possible	possível	poo-**see**-vel
post: ***by post***	pelo correio	**peh**-loo koo**rray**oo
to post	pôr no correio	pohr noo koo**rray**oo
post office	os correios	koo**rray**oosh
potato	a batata	bu**tah**-tuh
pound (money)	a libra	**lee**bruh
(weight)	= approx. 0.5 kilo	

P

English - Portuguese

power	o poder	poo**dehr**
to prefer	preferir	preh-fe**reer**
pregnant	grávida	**grah**-veeduh
I'm pregnant	estou grávida	shto **grah**-veeduh
to prepare	preparar	preh-pa**rar**
prescription	a receita médica	ruh-**say**-tuh **med**eekuh
present (gift)	o presente; a oferta; a prenda	pruh-**zeñt**; oo**fehr**tuh; **prayn**-duh
pressure	a pressão	pruh**sowñ**
blood pressure	a tensão arterial	tayñ-**sowñ** artehr-**yahl**
tyre pressure	a pressão dos pneus	pruh**sowñ** doosh **pnay**-oosh
pretty	bonito(a)	boo**nee**too(uh)
price	o preço	**pray**-soo
price list	a lista de preços	**leesh**tuh duh **pray**-soosh
private	privado(a)	pree**vah**-doo(uh)
probably	provavelmente	proovavel**meñt**
problem	o problema	proo**bleh**-muh
no problem	não há problema	nowñ a proo**bleh**-muh
prohibited	proibido(a)	proee-**bee**doo(uh)
pronounce	pronunciar	pronoonsee**ar**
how is this pronounced?	como se pronuncia isto?	**koh**-moo suh pronoon-**see**-uh **eesh**too?
to provide	fornecer	foorne**ssehr**
public	público(a)	**poo**bleekoo(uh)
public holiday	o feriado	fuh-ree**ah**-doo
to pull	puxar	poo**shar**
purse	o porta-moedas	**por**tuh-**mway**-dush
to push	empurrar	eeñpoo**rrar**
to put	pôr	por
to put back	repor	ruh-**por**
pyjamas	o pijama	pee**zhah**-muh

Q

quality	a qualidade	kwalee**dahd**
quantity	a quantidade	kwuñtee**dahd**
to quarrel	discutir	deesh-koo**teer**
quarter	o quarto	**kwar**too
question	a pergunta	pehr-**goon**tuh
queue	a fila	**fee**luh
to queue	fazer fila	fa**zehr fee**luh
quick	rápido(a)	**rah**-peedoo(uh)
quickly	depressa	duh-**pre**ssuh
quiet (place)	sossegado(a)	soo-se**gah**-doo(uh)
a quiet room	um quarto tranquilo	ooñ **kwar**too truñ**kwee**loo
quite: ***it's quite good***	é bastante bom	e bush**tuñt** boñ
it's quite expensive	é muito caro	e **mweeñ**to **kah**-roo

R

radio	o rádio	**rah**-dyoo
railcard	o passe do comboio	**pass**uh **doo** koñ**boy**oo
railway	o caminho de ferro	kuh-**meen**-yoo duh **ferr**-oo
railway station	a estação de comboio	shtuh-**sowñ** duh koñ**boy**oo
rain	a chuva	**shoo**vuh
to rain: ***it's raining***	está a chover	shta a shoo**vehr**
raped: ***I've been raped***	fui violado(a)	fwee veeo**lah**-doo(uh)
rare (unique)	raro(a)	**rah**-roo(uh)
(steak)	mal passado(a)	mal puh-**sah**-doo(uh)
rate (price)	a taxa	**tash**uh
rate of exchange	o câmbio	**kuñ**byoo
raw	cru(a)	kroo(uh)
razor	a máquina de barbear	**mak**eenuh duh barbee**ar**
razor blades	as lâminas de barbear	**luh**meenush duh barbee**ar**
to read	ler	lehr

ready	pronto(a)	**proñ**-too(uh)
real	real	reh-**ahl**
to realize	perceber	pehr-suh-**behr**
reason	a razão	ruh-**zowñ**
receipt	o recibo	ruh-**see**boo
reception (desk)	a receção	ruh-se-**sowñ**
receptionist	o/a rececionista	ruh-sesyo-**neesh**-tuh
to recommend	recomendar	ruhkoomeñ**dar**
red	vermelho(a)	vehr-**mel**-yoo(uh)
to reduce	reduzir	ruh-doo**zeer**
reduction	o desconto	deesh**koñ**too
to refer to	referir-se a	ruh-fe**reer**-suh a
refund	o reembolso	ruh-ayñ-**bol**soo
to refuse	recusar	ruh-koo**zar**
to register (at hotel)	preencher o registo	pray-eñ**shehr** oo reh-**zheesh**too
registration form	a folha de registo	**fol**-yuh duh reh-**zheesh**too
to reimburse	reembolsar	ruh-embol**sar**
relation (family)	o/a parente	pa**reñt**
relationship (personal)	a relação	ruh-luh-**sowñ**
(family)	o parentesco	pareñ**tesh**koo
to remain	ficar	fee**kar**
to remember	lembrar-se de	laym**brar**-suh duh
I don't remember	não me lembro	nowñ muh **laym**broo
to remove	retirar	ruh-tee**rar**
rent (house)	a renda; o aluguer	**rayn**-duh; aloo**gehr**
(car)	o aluguer	aloo**gehr**
to rent (house, car)	alugar	aloo**gar**
repair	a reparação	ruh-paruh-**sowñ**
to repair	reparar; consertar	ruh-pa**rar**; koñsehr**tar**
to repeat	repetir	ruh-pe**teer**
to report (crime, person)	comunicar	komoonee**kar**
to request	pedir	pe**deer**
to require	precisar de	preh-see**zar** duh
reservation	a reserva	ruh-**zehr**vuh
to reserve	reservar	ruh-zehr**var**
reserved	reservado(a)	ruh-zehr**vah**-doo

rest (repose)	o descanso	deesh-**kuñ**soo
(remainder)	o resto	**resh**-too
the rest of the wine	o resto do vinho	oo **resh**-too doo **veen**-yoo
to rest	descansar	deesh-kuñ**sar**
restaurant	o restaurante	rushtoh-**ruñt**
to retire	reformar-se	ruh-foor**mar**-suh
retired	reformado(a)	ruh-foor**mah**-doo(uh)
I'm retired	estou reformado(a)	shto ruh-foor**mah**-doo(uh)
to return (to go back)	voltar	vol**tar**
(to give something back)	devolver	duh-vol**vehr**
return ticket	o bilhete de ida e volta	beel-**yet dee**duh ee **vol**tuh
rice	o arroz	a**rrosh**
rich (person)	rico(a)	**ree**koo(uh)
right (correct)	certo(a)	**sehr**-too(uh)
to be right	ter razão	tehr ruh-**zowñ**
right: ***on/to the right***	à direita	a dee-**ray**-tuh
ring (for finger)	o anel	uh-**nel**
to ring (bell)	tocar	too**kar**
(phone)	telefonar	tuh-luh-fo**nar**
it's ringing	está a tocar	shta a too**kar**
road	a estrada	**shtrah**-duh
road map	o mapa das estradas	**mah**-puh dush **shtrah**-dush
road sign	o sinal de trânsito	see**nahl** duh **truñ**zeetoo
roadworks	as obras na estrada	ush obrush nuh **shtrah**-duh
roast	assado(a)	uh-**ssah**doo(uh)
roll (bread)	o pãozinho	powñ**zeen**-yoo
romantic	romântico(a)	ro**muñ**teekoo(uh)
room (in house, hotel)	o quarto	**kwar**too
(space)	o espaço	eesh-**pah**-ssoo

R

English - Portuguese

room number	o número do quarto	**noo**meroo doo **kwar**too
room service	o serviço de quarto	ser**vee**soo duh **kwar**too
to run	correr	koo**rrehr**

S

sad	triste	treesht
safe (for valuables)	o cofre	kofr
safe	seguro(a)	se**goo**roo(uh)
is it safe?	é seguro?	e se**goo**roo?
safety belt	o cinto de segurança	**seeñ**-too duh segoo**ruñ**suh
salad	a salada	sah-**lah**-duh
salary	o salário	sa**lar**yoo
sale(s)	o saldo	**sal**doo
salesman/woman	o/a vendedor(a)	veñdeh-**dor**(uh)
salt	o sal	sal
same	mesmo(a)	**mesh**-moo(uh)
sand	a areia	a**ray**-uh
sandwich	a sandes	**suñ**dush
satellite TV	a televisão via satélite	tuh-luh-vee**zowñ** **vee**-uh suh-**teh**-leet
Saturday	o sábado	**sah**-buh-doo
sauce	o molho	**mol**-yoo
tomato sauce	o molho de tomate	**mol**-yoo duh to-**maht**
sausage	a salsicha	sal**see**shuh
to save (life)	salvar	sal**var**
(money)	poupar	poh-**par**
to say	dizer	dee**zehr**
scarf (woollen)	o cachecol	kashee**kol**
school	a escola	eesh-**ko**luh
Scotland	a Escócia	eesh-**koss**-yuh
Scottish	escocês (escocesa)	eesh-ko**saysh** (eesh-ko**say**-zuh)
sea	o mar	mar
seafood	os mariscos	ma**reesh**-koosh
to search for	procurar	prokoo**rar**
seasick	enjoado(a)	ayñ-zhoo**ah**-doo(uh)

I get seasick	fico enjoado(a)	**fee**koo ayñ-zhoo**ah**-doo(uh)
seaside	a praia	**pry**-uh
at the seaside	na praia	nuh **pry**-uh
season (of year)	a estação	shtuh-**sowñ**
(holiday)	a temporada	tayñpo**rah**-duh
in season	da época	duh **eh**-pookuh
seat (chair)	a cadeira	kuh-**day**-ruh
(on bus, train, etc.)	o lugar	loo**gar**
seatbelt	o cinto de segurança	**seeñ**-too duh segoo**ruñ**suh
second	segundo(a)	se**goon**doo(uh)
second-class adj	de segunda classe	duh suh**goon**-duh klass
to see	ver	vehr
to sell	vender	vayñ**dehr**
do you sell...?	vende...?	vayñd...?
to send	mandar	muñ**dar**
serious	sério(a)	**sehr**-yoo(uh)
(illness)	grave	grahv
to serve	servir	sehr-**veer**
service (in restaurant)	o serviço	ser**vee**soo
is service included?	o serviço está incluído?	oo ser**vee**soo shta eeñkloo-**ee**doo?
service charge	a taxa de serviço	**ta**sha duh ser**vee**soo
service station	a estação de serviço	shtuh-**sowñ** duh ser**vee**soo
several	vários(as)	**var**yoosh(ush)
sex (gender)	o sexo	**sek**soo
(intercourse)	o sexo	**sek**soo
shade	a sombra	**soñ**bruh
in the shade	à sombra	a **soñ**bruh
to shake (bottle)	sacudir	sakoo**deer**
shampoo	o champô	shuñ**poo**
to share	dividir	deevee**deer**
to shave	fazer a barba	fa**zehr** uh **bar**buh
she	ela	**ay**luh
sheet (for bed)	o lençol	layñ-**sol**
shellfish	o marisco	ma**reesh**-koo

S

English – Portuguese

S

English - Portuguese

shirt	a camisa	kuh-**mee**zuh
shoe	o sapato	suh-**pah**-too
shoe shop	a sapataria	sapuh-tuh-**ree**-uh
shop	a loja	**lo**zhuh
shop assistant	o/a vendedor(a)	veñdeh-**dor**(uh)
shopping centre	o centro comercial	**señ**troo komehr-**syahl**
short	curto(a)	**koor**too(uh)
shorts	os calções	oosh kal**soyñsh**
to shout	gritar	gree**tar**
show	o espetáculo	eesh-peh-**tak**ooloo
to show	mostrar	moosh-**trar**
shower	o duche; o chuveiro	doosh; shoo**vay**roo
(rain)	o aguaceiro	ugwuh-**say**roo
to have a shower	tomar um duche	too**mar** ooñ doosh
shut (closed)	fechado(a)	fuh-**shah**-doo(uh)
to shut	fechar	fuh-**shar**
sick (ill)	doente	doo-**eñt**
I feel sick	sinto-me maldisposto(a)	**seen**-too-muh maldeesh-**posh**too(uh)
side	o lado	**lah**-doo
side dish	o acompanha-mento	uh-koñpun-yuh-**meñ**too
sightseeing	o turismo	too**reezh**-moo
to go sightseeing	fazer turismo	fa**zehr** too**reezh**-moo
sightseeing tour	a excursão	eesh-koor-**sowñ**
sign (road-, notice, etc.)	o sinal	see**nahl**
to sign	assinar	assee**nar**
signature	a assinatura	asseenuh-**too**ruh
silver	a prata	**prah**tuh
similar: ***similar to***	semelhante a	semel-**yuñt** a
simple	simples	**seeñ**pleesh
since (time)	desde	dezhd
(because)	porque	**poor**kuh
since Saturday	desde sábado	dezhd **sah**-buh-doo
to sing	cantar	kuñ**tar**
single (not married)	solteiro(a)	sol**tay**-roo(uh)

(not double)	simples	**seeñ**pleesh
sir	senhor	sun-**yor**
sister	a irmã	eer**mañ**
to sit	sentar-se	sayñ-**tar**-suh
size (clothes)	o tamanho	tuh-**mun**-yoo
(shoes)	o número	**noo**meroo
skin	a pele	payl
skirt	a saia	**sy**-uh
sky	o céu	**say**-oo
to sleep	dormir	door**meer**
to sleep in	dormir até tarde	door**meer** uh-**te** tard
slow	lento(a)	**leñ**too(uh)
small	pequeno(a)	puh-**kay**noo(uh)
smaller	mais pequeno(a)	mysh puh-**kay**noo(uh)
smell	o cheiro	**shay**-roo
smoke	o fumo	**foo**moo
to smoke	fumar	foo**mar**
I don't smoke	não fumo	nowñ **foo**moo
can I smoke?	posso fumar?	**poss**oo foo**mar**?
smoking: *no smoking*	proibido fumar	proee-**bee**doo foo**mar**
smooth	liso(a); macio(a)	**lee**soo(uh); ma**ssee**oo(uh)
snack	o lanche	luñsh
to have a snack	comer qualquer coisa	ko**mehr** kwal**kehr** **koy**-zuh
snow	a neve	nev
to snow	nevar	neh-**var**
so	tão	towñ
so much	tanto(a)	**tuñ**too(uh)
so then	portanto	poor**tuñ**too
soap	o sabão	sah-**bowñ**
sober	sóbrio(a)	**so**breeoo
socket (electrical)	a tomada	too**mah**-duh
sofa	o sofá	soo**fah**
soft	macio(a)	ma**ssee**oo(uh)
soft drink	o refrigerante	ruh-freezhe**ruñt**
some	alguns (algumas)	al**goonsh** (al**goo**mush)
someone	alguém	al**gayñ**

something	alguma coisa	al**goo**muh **koy**-zuh
sometimes	às vezes	ash **veh**-zush
son	o filho	**feel**-yoo
song	a canção	kuñ**sowñ**
soon	em breve	ayñ brev
as soon as possible	o mais rápido possível	oo **mysh rah**-peedoo poo-**see**-vel
sore	dorido(a)	doo**ree**doo(uh)
sore throat: ***I have a sore throat***	dói-me a garganta	**doy**-muh a gar**guñ**tuh
sorry: ***I'm sorry!***	lamento; desculpe!	luh-**mayn**too: dush**koolp**!
soup	a sopa	**so**puh
sour	azedo(a)	uh-**zeh**-doo(uh)
south	o sul	sool
souvenir	a recordação	ruh-koorduh-**sowñ**
Spain	a Espanha	eesh-**pun**-yuh
Spanish	espanhol(a)	eesh-pun-**yol** (eesh-pun-**yol**uh)
(language)	o espanhol	eespun-**yol**
sparkling	espumoso(a)	eespoo**mo**zoo(uh)
sparkling water	a água com gás	**ahg**-wuh koñ gahs
sparkling wine	o espumante	eespoo**muñt**
to speak	falar	fa**lar**
do you speak English?	fala inglês?	**fah**-luh eeñ**glaysh**?
I don't speak Portuguese	não falo português	nowñ **fah**-loo poortoo-**gaysh**
special	especial	eesh-pess**yahl**
speciality	a especialidade	shpuh-syalee-**dahd**
speed	a velocidade	velossee**dahd**
speeding	o excesso de velocidade	eh-**seh**-soo duh velossee**dahd**
speed limit	o limite de velocidade	lee**meet** duh velossee**dahd**
spell: ***how do you spell it?***	como se escreve?	**koh**-moo suh shkrev?
to spend (money)	gastar	gash-**tar**
spicy	picante	pee**kuñt**
to spill	entornar	eñtor**nar**

spirits	as bebidas alcoólicas	be **bee**dush al**ko**leekush
spoon	a colher	kohl-**yer**
sport	o desporto	deesh-**por**too
sports shop	a loja de artigos desportivos	**lo**zhuh duh ar**tee**goosh deesh-por**tee**voosh
spring (season)	a primavera	preemuh-**vehr**uh
(coil)	a mola	**mo**luh
square (in town)	a praça	**prass**uh
squash (drink)	o sumo	**soo**moo
(game)	o squash	skwosh
stadium	o estádio	**shtah**dyoo
staff	o pessoal	puh-**swahl**
stain	a nódoa	**no**doh-uh
stairs	a escada	eesh**kah**-duh
stamp (postage)	o selo	**se**loo
to stand	estar em pé	esh-**tar** ayñ pe
to stand up	levantar-se	leh-vuñ**tar**-suh
star (in sky, in films)	a estrela	eesh**tre**luh
to start	começar	koome**ssar**
starter (in meal)	a entrada	eñ**trah**-duh
(in car)	o motor de arranque	moo**tor** duh a**rruñk**
station	a estação	shtuh-**sowñ**
statue	a estátua	**shtah**too-uh
stay	a estadia; a visita	shta**dee**-uh; vee**zee**tuh
to stay	ficar	fee**kar**
I'm staying at a hotel	fico num hotel	**fee**koo nooñ oh-**tel**
steak	o bife	beef
medium steak	o bife ao ponto	beef ow **poñ**too
well-done steak	o bife bem-passado	beef bayñ-puh-**sah**-doo
rare steak	o bife malpassado	beef malpuh-**sah**-doo
to steal	roubar	ro-**bar**
to steam	cozer no vapor	ko**zehr** noo vuh-**por**
step (stair)	o degrau	deh-**gra**-oo
stereo	o estéreo	**shte**-ryo

S

English - Portuguese

sterling (pounds)	esterlino(a)	eesh-tehr-**lee**noo(uh)
still (not moving)	imóvel	ee**mo**vel
(not sparkling)	sem gás	sayñ gahs
(yet)	ainda	a-**eeñ**duh
stolen	roubado(a)	roh-**bah**-doo(uh)
stomach	o estômago	**shtoh**-muh-goo
stomach upset	o mal-estar de estômago	mal esh-**tar** duh**shtoh**-muh-goo
stone	a pedra	**pe**druh
(weight)	= approx. 6.5 kg	
to stop (come to a halt)	parar	pa**rar**
(stop doing something)	deixar de (fazer alguma coisa)	day-**shar** duh (fa**zehr** al**goo**muh **koy**-zuh)
store (shop)	a loja	**lo**zhuh
storey	o andar	uñ**dar**
storm	a tempestade	teñp-**shtahd**
story	a história	eesh**tor**-yuh
straightaway	imediatamente	eemuh-dee-ah-tuh-**meñt**
straight on	sempre em frente	**sayñ**pruh ayñ freñt
strange	estranho(a)	eesh-**trun**-yoo(uh)
strawberry	o morango	moo**ruñ**goo
street	a rua	**roo**-uh
street map	o mapa da cidade	**mah**-puh duh seedahd
strength	a força	**for**ssuh
strong	forte	fort
strong coffee	o café forte	kuh-**fe** fort
strong tea	o chá forte	shah fort
student	o/a estudante	shtoo**duñt**
student discount	o desconto para estudantes	deesh**koñ**too **pa**ruh shtoo**duñ**tush
stung	picado(a)	pee**kah**-doo(uh)
suddenly	de repente	duh ruh-**peñt**
sugar	o açúcar	uh-**soo**kar
sugar-free	sem açúcar	sayñ uh-**soo**kar
to suggest	sugerir	soozhe**reer**
suit (men's and women's)	o fato; o conjunto	**fah**-too; koñ**zhoon**too

suitcase	a mala	**mah**-luh
sum	a soma	**so**muh
summer	o verão	vuh-**rowñ**
sun	o sol	sol
to sunbathe	tomar banhos de sol	too**mar bun**-yoosh duh sol
sunblock	o protetor solar	prote**tor** so**lar**
sunburn	a queimadura de sol	kaymuh-**doo**ruh duh sol
Sunday	o domingo	doo**meen**goo
sunglasses	os óculos de sol	**oh**-kooloosh duh sol
sunny: ***it's sunny***	está sol	shta sol
sunrise	o nascer do sol	nash-**sehr** doo sol
sunshade	o guarda-sol; o toldo	**gwar**duh-sol; **tol**doo
sunstroke	a insolação	eeñsoluh-**sowñ**
suntan	o bronzeado	broñ-zeh-**ah**-doo
supermarket	o supermercado	sooper-mer**kah**-doo
supper	a ceia	**say**-uh
sure	seguro(a)	se**goo**roo(uh)
I'm sure	tenho a certeza	**ten**-yoo uh suhr**teh**za
surname	o apelido	apee**lee**doo
my surname is...	o meu apelido é...	may**oo** apee**lee**doo e...
surprise	a surpresa	soor**pre**zuh
to survive	sobreviver	sobruh-vee**vehr**
to swear (bad language)	blasfemar; praguejar	blashfe**mar**; pruh-ge**zhar**
(in court)	jurar	zhoo**rar**
to sweat	suar	soo**ar**
sweet (not savoury)	doce	dohss
sweetener	o adoçante	adoh**ssuñt**
to swell (injury etc.)	inchar	eeñ**shar**
to swim	nadar	nuh-**dar**
swimming pool	a piscina	peesh-**see**nuh
swimsuit	o fato de banho	**fah**-too duh **bun**-yoo
to switch off	apagar; desligar	apuh-**gar**; desh-lee**gar**
to switch on	acender; ligar	asseñ**dehr**; lee**gar**

swollen (finger, ankle, etc.)	inchado(a)	eeñ**shah**-doo(uh)

T

table	a mesa	**may**-zuh
tablet (pill)	o comprimido	koñpree**mee**doo
table tennis	o ping-pong	peeñg-poñg
table wine	o vinho de mesa	**veen**-yoo duh **may**-zuh
take (carry)	levar; transportar	luh-**var**; truñspoor**tar**
(to grab, seize)	agarrar	aga**rrar**
(medicine etc.)	tomar	too**mar**
(to take someone to)	levar	luh-**var**
how long does it take?	quanto tempo demora?	**kwuñ**too **tayñ**-poo duh-**mor**-uh?
take-away (food)	para levar	**pa**ruh luh-**var**
to take off (aircraft)	levantar voo	leh-vuñ**tar voh**-oo
to take out (of bag etc.)	tirar	tee**rar**
to talk to	conversar com	koñvehr**sar** koñ
tall	alto(a)	**ahl**too(uh)
tart	a tarte	tart
taste	o sabor	suh-**bor**
to taste	provar	proo**var**
can I taste it?	posso provar?	**poss**oo proo**var**?
tax	o imposto	eeñ**posh**-too
taxi	o táxi	**tak**see
tea	o chá	shah
lemon tea	o chá de limão	shah duh lee**mowñ**
tea with milk	o chá com leite	shah koñ layt
to teach	ensinar	ayñ-see**nar**
teacher	o/a professor(a)	proofe**ssor**(uh)
team	a equipa	e**kee**puh
teeth	os dentes	oosh **deñ**tush
telephone	o telefone	tuh-luh-**fo**nee
to telephone	telefonar	tuh-luh-fo**nar**
telephone box	a cabine telefónica	ku**been** tuh-luh-**fo**neekuh
telephone call	a chamada	shah-**mah**-duh

telephone directory	a lista telefónica	**leesh**tuh tuh-luh-**fo**neekuh
telephone number	o número de telefone	**noo**meroo duh tuh-luh-**fo**nee
television	a televisão	tuh-luh-vee**zowñ**
to tell	dizer	dee**zehr**
temperature	a temperatura	teñpruh-**too**ruh
to have a temperature	ter febre	tehr **feb**ruh
temporary	temporário(a)	tayñpo**rah**-reeoo(uh)
tennis	o ténis	**teh**-neesh
to test (try out)	testar	tesh-**tar**
than	do que	doo kuh
better than	melhor do que	mel-**yor** doo kuh
more than you	mais do que tu	mysh doo kuh too
more than five	mais de cinco	mysh duh **seeñ**koo
to thank	agradecer	uh-grade**ssehr**
thank you/thanks	obrigado(a)	oh-bree**gah**-doo (-duh)
thank you very much	muito obrigado(a)	**mweeñ**to oh-bree**gah**-doo (-duh)
no thanks	não, obrigado(a)	nowñ, oh-bree**gah**-doo(duh)
that	aquele (aquela)	uh-**kayl** (uh-**kel**uh)
the (sing)	o (a)	oo (uh)
(plural)	os (as)	oosh (ush)
theatre	o teatro	tee-**ah**-troo
theft	o roubo	**roh**-boo
their	seu (sua)	**say**oo (**soo**-uh)
them (direct object)	os (as)	oosh (ush)
(indirect object)	lhes	lyesh
(after preposition)	eles (elas)	**ay**lush (**el**ush)
then	então	ayñ-**towñ**
there (over there)	ali	a**lee**
there is/there are	há	a
these	estes (estas)	**aysh**tesh (**aysh**tush)
these ones	estes (estas)	**aysh**tesh (**aysh**tush)
they	eles (elas)	**ay**lush (**el**ush)
thick	grosso(a)	**gro**ssoo(uh)

T

English - Portuguese

thin	magro(a)	**mag**roo(uh)
thing	a coisa	**koy**-zuh
my things	as minhas coisas	**meen**-yush **koy**-zush
to think	pensar	peñ**sar**
(to be of opinion)	achar	uh-**shar**
thirsty: *I'm thirsty*	tenho sede	**ten**-yoo sehd
this	este (esta)	**aysh**t (**aysh**tuh)
this one	este (esta)	**aysh**t (**aysh**tuh)
those	aqueles (aquelas)	uh-**kay**lush (uh-**kel**ush)
those ones	aqueles (aquelas)	uh-**kay**lush (uh-**kel**ush)
throat	a garganta	gar**guñ**tuh
through	através de	atruh-**vesh** duh
to throw away	deitar fora; descartar	day-**tar for**-uh; deesh-kar**tar**
thunderstorm	o temporal; a tempestade	tayñpoo**rahl**; tayñp-**shtahd**
Thursday	a quinta-feira	**keeñ**tuh-**fay**ruh
ticket (bus, train)	o bilhete	beel-**yet**
(for cinema, theatre etc.)	a entrada	eñ**trah**-duh
a single ticket	um bilhete de ida	ooñ beel-**yet dee**duh
a return ticket	um bilhete de ida e volta	ooñ beel-**yet dee**duh ee **vol**tuh
ticket office	a bilheteira	beel-yeh-**tay**ruh
tidy	arrumado(a)	arroo**mah**-doo(uh)
to tidy up	arrumar	arroo**mar**
tie	a gravata	gruh-**vah**tuh
tight	apertado(a)	apehr**tah**-doo(uh)
tile (floor)	o ladrilho	luh-**dreel**-yoo
(wall)	o azulejo	azoo**lay**zhoo
till (cash desk)	a caixa	**ky**-shuh
till (until)	até	uh-**te**
till 2 o'clock	até às duas	uh-**te** ash **doo**-ush
time	o tempo	**tayñ**poo
(clock)	as horas	ush **or**uz
what time is it?	que horas são?	kee **or**uz sowñ?
this time	esta vez	**esh**tuh vesh
timetable	o horário	oh-**rar**yoo

tip	a gorjeta	goor**zhe**tuh
to tip	dar uma gorjeta	dar **oo**muh goor**zhe**tuh
tired	cansado(a)	kuñ**sah**-doo(uh)
to	a	a
to the airport	ao aeroporto	ow uh-ayroo-**por**too
toast (to eat)	a torrada	too**rrah**-duh
(raising glass)	o brinde	oo breeñd
tobacco	o tabaco	ta**bah**-koo
tobacconist's	a tabacaria	tabakuh-**ree**-uh
today	hoje	ohzh
together	juntos	**zhoon**toosh
toilet	a casa de banho; o lavabo	**kah**-zuh duh **bun**-yoo; luh-**vah**-boo
disabled toilets	a casa de banho para deficientes	**kah**-zuh duh **bun**-yoo **pa**ruh duh-feess-**yeñtsh**
toilet paper	o papel higiénico	puh-**pel** ee-zhee-**eh**-nee-koo
toll (motorway)	a portagem	por**tah**-zhayñ
tomato	o tomate	to-**maht**
tomato juice	o sumo de tomate	**soo**moo duh to-**maht**
tomato sauce	o molho de tomate	**mo**l-yoo duh to-**maht**
tomorrow	amanhã	amun-**yañ**
tomorrow morning	amanhã de manhã	amun-**yañ** duh mun-**yañ**
tomorrow afternoon	amanhã à tarde	amun-**yañ** a tard
tomorrow evening	amanhã ao fim da tarde/à noite	amun-**yañ** ow feeñ duh tard/a noyt
tomorrow night	amanhã à noite	amun-**yañ** a noyt
tonic water	a água tónica	**ahg**-wuh **to**neekuh
tonight	esta noite	**esh**tuh noyt
too (also)	também	tuñ**bayñ**
too big	grande demais	gruñd duh-**mysh**
too small	pequeno(a) demais	puh-**kay**noo(uh) duh-**mysh**

too noisy	demasiado barulhento(a)	demaz**yah**doo barool-**yeñ**too(uh)
tooth	o dente	deñt
top: ***the top floor***	o último andar	**ool**teemoo uñ**dar**
on top of...	em cima de...	ayñ **see**muh duh...
total (amount)	o total	too**tahl**
to touch	tocar	to**kar**
tour (trip)	a excursão	eeshkoor**sowñ**
(of museum etc.)	a visita	vee**zee**tuh
guided tour	a visita guiada	vee**zee**tuh ghee-**ah**-duh
tour guide	o/a guia turístico(a)	**ghee**-uh too**reesh**teekoo(uh)
tour operator	a empresa de viagens	eñ**preh**-zuh duhvee-**ah**-zhayñsh
tourist	o/a turista	too**reesh**tuh
tourist information	a informação turística	eeñfoormuh-**sowñ** too**reesh**teekuh
tourist office	o posto de turismo	**posh**-too duh too**reezh**-moo
town	a cidade	see**dahd**
town centre	o centro da cidade	**señ**troo duh see**dahd**
town hall	a Câmara Municipal	**kum**uh-ruh mooneesee**pahl**
town plan	o mapa da cidade	**mah**-puh duh see**dahd**
toxic	tóxico(a)	**tok**seekoo(uh)
toy	o brinquedo	breeñ**keh**-doo
toy shop	a loja de brinquedos	**lo**zhuh duh breeñ**keh**-doosh
traditional	tradicional	truh-deessyo**nahl**
traffic	o trânsito	**truñ**zeetoo
traffic jam	o engarrafamento	eeñgarrufuh-**meñ**too
traffic lights	o semáforo	se**mah**-fooroo
traffic warden	o/a polícia de trânsito	poo**leess**-yuh duh **truñ**zeetoo
train	o comboio	koñ**boy**oo
by train	de comboio	duh koñ**boy**oo
the next train	o próximo comboio	**pross**eemoo koñ**boy**oo

the first train	o primeiro comboio	pree**may**-roo koñ**boy**oo
the last train	o último comboio	**ool**teemoo koñ**boy**oo
tram	o elétrico	e**le**treekoo
to transfer	transferir	truñsfe**reer**
to translate	traduzir	tradoo**zeer**
translation	a tradução	tradoo**sowñ**
to travel	viajar	veeuh-**zhar**
travel agent	o agente de viagens	uh-**zheñt** duh vee-**ah**-zhayñsh
travel insurance	o seguro de viagem	se**goo**roo duh vee-**ah**-zhayñ
trip	a viagem	vee-**ah**-zhayñ
trolley (luggage, shopping)	o carrinho	kuh-**reen**-yoo
trouble	os problemas	proo**bleh**-mush
to be in trouble	estar em dificuldades	esh-**tar** ayñ deefeekool**dah**-dush
trousers	as calças	**kahl**ssush
true	verdadeiro(a)	vehr-duh-**day**roo(uh)
to try (attempt)	tentar	tayñ-**tar**
to try on (clothes, shoes)	provar	proo**var**
T-shirt	a T-shirt	t-shirt
Tuesday	a terça-feira	**tehr**-suh-**fay**ruh
to turn	voltar; girar	vol**tar**; zhee**rar**
to turn around	voltar-se	vol**tar**-suh
to turn off (light)	apagar	apuh-**gar**
(engine)	desligar	desh-lee**gar**
(tap)	fechar	fuh-**shar**
to turn on (light)	acender	asseñ**dehr**
(engine)	ligar	lee**gar**
(tap)	abrir	uh-**breer**
twice	duas vezes	**doo**-ush **veh**-zush
twin-bedded room	o quarto com duas camas	**kwar**too koñ **doo**-ush **ku**mush
typical	típico	**tee**peekoo

U

English	Portuguese	Pronunciation
ugly	feio(a)	**fay**-oo(uh)
umbrella	o guarda-chuva	**gwar**duh **shoo**vuh
(sunshade)	o guarda-sol	**gwar**duh-sol
uncomfortable	incómodo(a)	eeñ**koñ**odoo(uh)
under	debaixo de	duh-**by**-shoo duh
underground (metro)	o metropolitano	metropoleet**uh**-noo
to understand	compreender	koñpreh-ayñ-**dehr**
I don't understand	não percebo	nowñ pehr-**seh**boo
do you understand?	percebe?	pehr-**sehb**-ee?
underwear	a roupa interior	**roh**-puh eeñtehr-**yor**
to undress	despir-se	dush-**peer**-suh
unemployed	desempregado(a)	duh-zaympreh-**gah**-doo(uh)
United Kingdom	o Reino Unido	**ray**-noo oo**nee**doo
United States	os Estados Unidos	eesh-**tah**dooz oo-**nee**doosh
to unlock	destrancar	deesh-truñ**kar**
to unpack (suitcases)	desfazer as malas	deesh-fa**zehr** ush **mal**ush
unpleasant	desagradável	dezagruh-**dah**vel
(person)	antipático(a)	uñtee**pah**teekoo(uh)
until	até	uh-**te**
until 2 o'clock	até às duas	uh-**te** ash **doo**-ush
unusual	invulgar	eeñvool**gar**
up: ***to get up***	levantar-se	leh-vuñ**tar**-suh
urgent	urgente	oor-**zheñt**
us	nos	noosh
(after preposition)	nós	nosh
to use	utilizar	ooteelee**zar**
useful	útil	**oo**teel
usual	habitual	abeet**wahl**
usually	geralmente	zhehral**meñt**

V

vacancies (in hotel etc.)	os quartos vagos	**kwar**toosh **vah**-goosh
(jobs)	as vagas	**vah**-gush
vacant	livre	**lee**-vree
(hotel room)	vago(a)	**vah**-goo(uh)
vacation	as férias	**fehr**-yush
on vacation	de férias	duh **fehr**-yush
valid	válido(a)	**vah**-leedoo(uh)
valuable	valioso(a)	valee-**o**zoo(uh)
valuables	os objetos de valor	ob**zhe**toosh duh va**lor**
value	o valor	va**lor**
VAT	o IVA	**ee**vah
vegan	vegan	**veh**gan
I'm vegan	sou vegan	soh **veh**gan
vegetables	os legumes; os vegetais	le**goo**mush; veh-zhuh-**tysh**
vegetarian	vegetariano(a)	veh-zhuh-tuh-**ryah**-noo(uh)
I'm vegetarian	sou vegetariano(a)	soh veh-zhuh-tuh-**ryah**-noo(uh)
very	muito	**mweeñ**too
video camera	a câmara de vídeo	**kum**uh-ruh duh**vee**-dee-oo
view	a vista	**veesh**-tuh
village	a aldeia	al-**day**-uh
vinegar	o vinagre	vee**nahg**ruh
visa	o visto	**veesh**too
visit	a visita	vee**zeet**uh
to visit	visitar	veezee**tar**
visitor	o/a visitante	veezee**tañt**
to vomit	vomitar	voomee**tar**
voucher	o vale; o recibo	val; reh-**see**boo

W

to wait for	esperar por	eesh-peh-**rar** poor
waiter/waitress	o/a empregado(a) de mesa	ayñpreh-**gah**-doo(duh) duh **may**-zuh
waiting room	a sala de espera	**sah**-luh duh **shpeh**-ruh
to wake up	acordar	akoor**dar**
Wales	o País de Gales	pah-**eesh** duh **gal**eesh
to walk	andar	uñ**dar**
walk	o passeio	puh-**say**-oo
wall (inside)	a parede	pa**red**
(outside)	o muro	**moo**roo
wallet	a carteira	kar-**tay**-ruh
to want	querer	kay**rehr**
I want...	quero...	**kay**roo...
we want...	queremos...	kay**reh**moosh...
warm	quente	keñt
I'm warm	estou com calor	shto koñ ka**lor**
it's warm (weather)	está calor	shta ka**lor**
to warm up	aquecer	akuh-**sehr**
to wash	lavar	la**var**
watch	o relógio	ruh-**lozh**-yoo
water	a água	**ahg**-wuh
sparkling water	a água com gás	**ahg**-wuh koñ gahs
still water	a água sem gás	**ahg**-wuh sayñ gahs
watermelon	a melancia	meluñ**see**-uh
way in (entrance)	a entrada	eñ**trah**-duh
way out (exit)	a saída	sah-**ee**duh
we	nós	nosh
weak	fraco(a)	**frah**koo(uh)
(tea, etc.)	aguado(a)	ug-**wah**-doo(uh)
to wear	vestir	veesh**teer**
weather	o tempo	**tayñ**-poo
weather forecast	a previsão do tempo	preh-vee**zowñ** doo **tayñ**-poo
wedding	o casamento	kuzuh-**mayñ**-too
Wednesday	a quarta-feira	**kwar**tuh-**fay**ruh

week	a semana	suh-**mah**-nuh
last week	a semana passada	uh suh-**mah**-nuh puh-**sah**-duh
next week	a semana que vem	uh suh-**mah**-nuh kuh vayñ
per week	por semana	poor suh-**mah**-nuh
this week	esta semana	**esh**tuh suh-**mah**-nuh
weekend	o fim de semana	feeñ duh suh-**mah**-nuh
next weekend	o próximo fim de semana	oo **pross**eemoo feeñ duh suh-**mah**-nuh
this weekend	este fim de semana	aysht feeñ duh suh-**mah**-nuh
weekly	por semana	poor suh-**mah**-nuh
weekly ticket	o bilhete semanal	beel-**yet** suh-muh-**nahl**
to weigh	pesar	peh-**zar**
weight	o peso	**peh**-zoo
welcome	bem-vindo(a)	bayñ-**veeñ**-doo(uh)
well	bem	bayñ
he's not well	ele não se sente bem	ayl nowñ suh señt bayñ
Welsh	galês (galesa)	ga**laysh** (ga**lay**-zuh)
(language)	o galês	ga**laysh**
west	o oeste	o**ay**sht
wet	molhado(a)	mool-**yah**-doo(uh)
(weather)	chuvoso(a)	shoo**vo**zoo(uh)
what	que	kuh
what is it?	o que é?	kuh e?
when?	quando?	**kwuñ**doo?
where?	onde?	**oñ**duh?
which: ***which is it?***	qual é?	kwal e?
while	enquanto	ayñ-**kwuñ**too
in a while	daqui a pouco	duh-**kee** uh **poh**koo
white	branco(a)	**bruñ**koo(uh)
who: ***who is it?***	quem é?	kayñ e?
whole	inteiro(a)	eeñ-**tay**-roo(uh)
wholemeal bread	o pão integral	powñ eeñteh-**grahl**

whose: ***whose is it?***	de quem é?	duh kayñ e?
why?	porquê?	poor-**keh**?
wide	largo(a)	**lar**goo(uh)
width	a largura	lar**goo**ruh
wife	a mulher; a esposa	mool-**yehr**; sh**po**zuh
to win	ganhar	gun-**yar**
wind	o vento	**veñ**too
window	a janela	zhuh-**ne**luh
(shop)	a montra	**moñ**truh
wine	o vinho	**veen**-yoo
red wine	o vinho tinto	**veen**-yoo **teeñ**too
white wine	o vinho branco	**veen**-yoo **bruñ**koo
rosé wine	o vinho rosé	**veen**-yoo roh-**ze**
dry wine	o vinho seco	**veen**-yoo **seh**-koo
sparkling wine	o vinho espumante	**veen**-yoo eesh-poo**muñt**
winter	o inverno	eeñ**vehr**-noo
with	com	koñ
with ice	com gelo	koñ **zhe**loo
without	sem	sayñ
without sugar	sem açúcar	sayñ uh-**soo**kar
woman	a mulher	mool-**yehr**
word	a palavra	pa**lah**-vruh
to work (person)	trabalhar	trabal-**yar**
(machine)	funcionar	foonss-yo**nar**
it doesn't work	não está a funcionar; não funciona	nowñ shta uh foonss-yo**nar**; nowñ foonss-**yo**nuh
world	o mundo	**moon**doo
worried	preocupado(a)	preh-okoo**pah**-doo(uh)
worse	pior	pee-**or**
to wrap (parcel)	embrulhar	ayñbrool-**yar**
to write	escrever	eesh-kreh-**vehr**
please write it down	escreva-o por favor	eesh-**kreh**-vuh-oo poor fuh-**vor**
wrong	errado(a)	e**rrah**-doo(uh)

X

x-ray	a radiografia	rah-dyoo-gra**fee**-uh
to x-ray	radiografar	rah-dyoo-gra**far**

Y

year	o ano	**ah**-noo
last year	o ano passado	**ah**-noo puh-**sah**-doo
next year	o ano que vem	**ah**-noo kuh vayñ
this year	este ano	aysht **ah**-noo
yearly: ***twice yearly***	duas vezes por ano	**doo**-ush **veh**-zush poor **ah**-noo
yellow	amarelo(a)	ama**reh**-loo(uh)
Yellow Pages®	as Páginas Amarelas®	ush **pah**-zheenush ama**reh**-lush
yes	sim	seeñ
yesterday	ontem	**oñ**-tayñ
yet: ***not yet***	ainda não	a-**eeñ**duh nowñ
you	você/tu/vocês/vós	voh-**say**/too/ voh-**saysh**/vosh
young	novo(a)	**noh**-voo(uh)
(person)	o/a jovem	**zho**vayñ
your	seu (sua)/teu (tua)/ seu (sua)/vosso(a)	**say**oo (**soo**-uh)/ **tay**oo (**too**-uh)/ **say**oo (**soo**-uh)/ **voss**oo(uh)
youth hostel	o albergue da juventude	al**behr**-guh duhzhuvayñ**tood**

Z

zone	a zona	**zo**nuh
zoo	o jardim zoológico	zhuhr**deeñ** zoh-o**lo**zheekoo

A

a	to; the *(feminine)*
abaixo	down; below
aberto	open
aberto todo o ano	open all year round
abril *m*	April
abrir	to open; to unlock *(door)*
acabar	to end; to finish
aceitar	to accept
achar	to think; to find
acha bem?	do you think it's all right?
acima	above
acordo *m*	agreement
Açores *mpl*	the Azores
actual	present(-day)
açúcar *m*	sugar
adega *f*	wine cellar
adeus *m*	goodbye
adiantado(a)	fast *(watch)*; early *(train, etc.)*
advogado(a) *m/f*	lawyer
aéreo(a): ***a linha aérea***	airline
via aérea	air mail
agora	now
agosto *m*	August
agradável	pleasant
agradecer	to thank
água *f*	water
aguardente *f*	spirit brandy
ajudar	to help
albergue *m*	hostel
albergue da juventude	youth hostel
alegre	jolly
alface *f*	lettuce
alfândega *f*	customs
algum(a)	some; any
alguns (algumas)	a few; some

mais alguma coisa?	anything else?
alho *m*	garlic
alho-francês *m*	leek
ali	there
almoço *m*	lunch
pequeno-almoço	breakfast
alto!	stop!
alto(a)	high; tall; loud
a estação alta	high season
altura *f*	height
alugar	to hire; to rent
aluga-se	to rent
alugam-se quartos	rooms to let
aluguer *m*	rental
amanhã	tomorrow
amarelo(a)	yellow
amargo(a)	bitter
amêijoa *f*	clam; cockle
amigo(a) *m/f*	friend
analgésico *m*	painkiller
ananás *m*	pineapple
andar	to walk
andar *m*	floor; storey
o primeiro andar	first floor
aniversário *m*	anniversary; birthday
ano *m*	year
Ano Novo	New Year
antes (de)	before
apagar	to switch/turn off *(light, etc.)*
apelido *m*	surname
apelido de solteira	maiden name
apenas	only
apetite *m*	appetite
bom apetite!	enjoy your meal!
apólice de seguro *f*	insurance certificate
aquecedor *m*	heater; electric fire
aquecimento *m*	heating

aqui	here
ar *m*	air
ar condicionado	air conditioning
arder	to burn
areia *f*	sand
arroz *m*	rice
árvore *f*	tree
ascensor *m*	lift
assado(a)	roast; baked
assinar	to sign
assinatura *f*	signature
até	until; as far as
atrás	behind
atrasado(a)	late *(for appointment)*
atrasar	to delay
atravessar	to cross
atum *m*	tuna *(fish)*
autocarro *m*	bus; coach
a paragem de autocarro	bus stop
autoestrada *f*	motorway
autorização *f*	licence; permit
avariado(a)	out of order *(machine)*; broken down *(car)*
avião *m*	plane
aviso *m*	warning
avô *m*	grandfather
avó *f*	grandmother
azedo(a)	sour
azeite *m*	olive oil
azeitona *f*	olive
azul	blue
azulejo *m*	ornamental tile

B

bacalhau *m*	dried salt cod
bagagem *f*	luggage; baggage

baixo: ***em baixo***	below
balcão *m*	shop counter; circle in theatre
banco *m*	bank; seat *(in car, etc.)*
banho *m*	bath
a casa de banho	bathroom
tomar banho	to have a bath
barato(a)	cheap
barco *m*	boat; ship
barriga *f*	belly
barulho *m*	noise
bastante	enough
batata *f*	potato
bater	to beat; to knock
bata à porta	please knock
batido de leite *m*	milk shake
baunilha *f*	vanilla
bebé *m*	baby
beber	to drink
bebida *f*	drink
belo(a)	beautiful
bem	well
está bem	OK
bem passado	well done *(steak)*
bem-vindo(a)	welcome
berço *m*	crib; cradle; cot
bica *f*	espresso coffee
bicha *f*	queue
fazer bicha	to queue
bife *m*	steak
bife com batatas fritas	steak and chips
bilhete *m*	ticket; fare
bilhete de entrada	admission ticket
bilhete de identidade	identity card
bilheteira *f*	ticket office
boa	see **bom**
boca *f*	mouth

bola *f*	ball
bolacha *f*	biscuit
bolo *m*	cake
bolsa *f*	stock exchange; handbag
bom (boa)	good; fine *(weather)*; kind
bom dia	good morning
boa tarde	good afternoon
boa noite	good evening; good night
bombeiros *mpl*	fire brigade
bonito(a)	pretty
borrego *m*	lamb
bota *f*	boot *(to wear)*
braço *m*	arm
branco(a)	white
breve	brief
em breve	soon
britânico(a)	British
broa *f*	corn *(maize)* bread
bronzeador *m*	suntan oil
buscar	to look for

C

cabeça *f*	head
cabeleireiro(a) *m/f*	hairdresser
cabelo *m*	hair
cabine *f*	cabin; booth
cabine telefónica	phone box
cada	each; every
cadeira *f*	chair
cadeira de bebé	high chair; push chair
cadeira de rodas	wheelchair
café *m*	*(black)* coffee; café
cair	to fall; to fall over
caixa *f*	cash desk
caixa automática	cash machine
caixa do correio	letterbox

C

Portuguese – English

calar-se to stop talking; to keep silent
calçado *m* footwear
calças *fpl* trousers
calções *mpl* shorts
calções de banho swimming trunks
calcular to estimate; to calculate
calor *m* heat
cama *f* bed
cama de bebé cot
cama de casal double bed
cama de solteiro single bed
a roupa de cama bedding
câmara municipal *f* town hall
cambiar to exchange; to change money
câmbio *m* exchange rate
casa de câmbios *f* exchange bureau
camião *m* lorry
camioneta *f* coach
camisa *f* shirt
camisa de noite nightdress
campismo *m* camping
campo *m* field; countryside
cancelar to cancel
caneta *f* pen
cansaço *m* fatigue
cansado(a) tired
cantar to sing
cão *m* dog
capacete *m* crash helmet
capela *f* chapel
cara *f* face
caranguejo *m* crab
carioca *m* weak coffee
carioca de limão lemon infusion
carne *f* meat
carnes frias cold meats
caro(a) expensive

C

caro(a) amigo(a)	dear friend
carro *m*	car
carta *f*	letter
cartão *m*	card; business card
cartão de crédito	credit card
cartão de débito	debit card
cartão de embarque	boarding card
cartão garantia	cheque card
carteira *f*	wallet
carteirista *m*	pickpocket
casa *f*	home; house
casa de banho	toilet; bathroom
casaco *m*	jacket; coat
casado(a)	married
casal *m*	couple
casamento *m*	wedding
caso *m*	case
em caso de...	in case of...
castanho(a)	brown
castelo *m*	castle
catedral *f*	cathedral
causa *f*	cause
por causa de	because of
cavalheiro *m*	gentleman
cave *f*	cellar
cebola *f*	onion
cedo	early
cego(a)	blind
cem	one hundred
cenoura *f*	carrot
cêntimo *m*	cent
centro *m*	centre
centro da cidade	city centre
centro comercial	shopping centre
centro de saúde	health centre
cereja *f*	cherry

certeza *f*	certainty
ter a certeza	to be sure
certo(a)	right *(correct, accurate)*; certain
cerveja *f*	beer; lager
céu *m*	sky
chá *f*	tea
chamada *f*	telephone call
chamada gratuita	free call
chamada internacional	international call
chamada pagável no destino	reverse charge call
chamar	to call
charcutaria *f*	delicatessen
chave *f*	key
fechar à chave	to lock up
chefe *mf*	boss
chegadas *fpl*	arrivals
chegar	to arrive
cheio(a)	full
cheirar	to smell
cheiro *m*	smell
cheque *m*	cheque
cheque de viagem	traveller's cheque
levantar um cheque	to cash a cheque
churrasqueira *f*	barbecue restaurant
churrasco *m*	barbecue
chuva *f*	rain
cidade *f*	town; city
cigarro *m*	cigarette
cima: *em cima de*	on *(top of)*
cinto *m*	belt
cinto de salvação	lifebelt
cinto de segurança	seat belt
cinzento(a)	grey
claro(a)	light *(colour)*; bright
cobrar	to charge
cobrir	to cover

código *m*	code; dialling code
código postal	postcode
cofre *m*	safe
coisa *f*	thing
colégio *m*	private school
colete de salvação *m*	life jacket
com	with
comando *m*	TV remote control
comboio *m*	train
combustível *m*	fuel
começar	to begin; to start
comer	to eat
comida *f*	food
como	as; how
como disse?	I beg your pardon?
como está?	how are you?
companheiro(a) *m/f*	live-in partner
companhia (Cia.) *f*	company
completar	to complete
completo	no vacancies *(sign in hotel, etc.)*
compra *f*	purchase
ir às compras	to go shopping
comprar	to buy
compreender	to understand
comprimido *m*	pill; tablet
computador *m*	computer
concordar	to agree
condução *f*	driving
a carta de condução	driving licence
condutor *m*	driver; chauffeur
conduzir	to drive
conferir	to check
congelado(a)	frozen *(food)*
congelar	to freeze
não congelar	do not freeze
conhaque *m*	cognac

conhecer	to know *(person, place)*
consertos *mpl*	repairs
conservar	to keep; to preserve
conservar no frio	store in a cold place
constipação *f*	cold *(illness)*
consulta *f*	consultation; appointment
consultório *m*	surgery
consumir antes de...	best before... *(label on food)*
conta *f*	account; bill
conter	to contain
não contém...	does not contain...
contra	against
contrato *m*	contract
convidar	to invite; to ask *(invite)*
copo *m*	glass *(container)*
cor *f*	colour
coração *m*	heart
cordeiro *m*	lamb
corpo *m*	body
correio *m*	post office
pelo correio	by post
correr	to flow; to run *(person)*
cortar	to cut; to cut off
cortar e fazer brushing	to cut and blow-dry
corte *m*	cut
costeleta *f*	chop *(meat)*; cutlet
couve *f*	cabbage
couvert *m*	cover charge
cozinha *f*	kitchen
cozinhar	to cook
creme *m*	custard
creme de barbear	shaving cream
creme para bronzear	suntan cream
criança *f*	child
cru(a)	raw
cruzamento *m*	junction *(crossroads)*

cuidado *m*	care *(caution)*
cumprimento *m*	greeting
cumprimentos	regards
curso *m*	course
curto(a)	short
curva *f*	bend; turning; curve
curva perigosa	dangerous bend
custar	to cost
custo *m*	charge; cost

D

dano *m*	damage
dar	to give
dar prioridade	to give way
data *f*	date
data de nascimento	date of birth
de	of; from
debaixo de	under
deficiente	disabled
degrau *m*	step *(stair)*
deitar-se	to lie down
deixar	to let *(allow)*; to leave behind
delito *m*	crime
demais	too; too much; too many
demorado(a)	late
demorar	to delay
dente(s) *m*	tooth/teeth
dentro	inside
depois	after(wards)
depósito *m*	deposit *(in bank)*
depósito de bagagens	left-luggage
depósito da gasolina	petrol tank
depressa	quickly
desaparecido(a)	missing
descansar	to rest
descer	to go down

desculpe excuse me; sorry
desejar to desire; to wish
desligado(a) off *(engine, gas)*
desligar to hang up *(phone)*; to switch off *(engine, radio)*
desmaiar to faint
despesa *f* expense
desporto *m* sport
devagar slowly; slow down *(sign)*
dever: ***eu devo*** I must
devolver to give back; to return
dezembro *m* December
dia *m* day
dia de anos birthday
dias da semana weekdays
dia útil working day
diário daily
diarreia *f* diarrhoea
dieta *f* diet; special diet
diferença *f* difference
difícil difficult
digestão *f* digestion
diminuir to reduce
dinheiro *m* money; cash
direção *f* direction; address; steering
direita *f* right(-hand side)
à direita on the right
para a direita to the right
direito(a) straight; right(-hand)
Dto. on right-hand side *(address)*
direitos *mpl* duty *(tax)*; rights
disponível available
dívida *f* debt
dizer to say
dobro *m* double
doce *adj* sweet *(taste)*
doente ill; sick

doer to ache; to hurt
domicílio *m* residence
domingo *m* Sunday
dono(a) *m/f* owner
dona de casa housewife
dor *f* ache; pain
dormir to sleep
Dto. see **direito(a)**
duche *m* shower
duplo(a) double
durante during
durar to last
duro(a) hard; stiff; tough *(meat)*

E

e and
é he/she/it is; you are
ela she; her; it
elas they *(feminine)*
ele he; him; it
eles they *(masculine)*
elétrico *m* tram
eletrodomésticos *mpl* electrical appliances
em at; in *(with towns, countries)*; into
embaixada *f* embassy
ementa *f* menu
ementa fixa set menu
empregado(a) *m/f* waiter (waitress); maid; attendant *(at petrol station)*; assistant *(in shop)*; office worker
emprego *m* job; employment
empurrar to push
empurre push *(sign)*
encher to fill up; to pump; to pump up *(tyre)*

enchidos *mpl*	processed meats; sausages
encontrar	to meet; to find
encontro *m*	date; meeting
endereço *m*	address
ensopado *m*	stew served on slice of bread
enorme	big; huge
entender	to understand
entrada *f*	entrance; starter *(in meal)*
entrada livre	admission free
entrar	to go in; to come in; to get into *(car, etc.)*
entre	among; between
enviar	to send
enxaqueca *f*	migraine
erro *m*	mistake
ervilhas *fpl*	peas
escada *f*	ladder; stairs
escada rolante	escalator
escocês (escocesa)	Scottish
Escócia *f*	Scotland
escola *f*	school
escrever	to write
escritório *m*	office
escuro(a)	dark *(colour)*
escutar	to listen to
esgotado(a)	sold out *(tickets)*; exhausted
espaço *m*	space
Espanha *f*	Spain
espanhol *m*	Spanish *(language)*
espanhol(a)	Spanish
esparguete *m*	spaghetti
esperar	to expect; to hope
esperar por	to wait for
esposa *f*	wife
espumante *m*	sparkling wine
esquerda *f*	left(-hand side)
à esquerda	on the left

Portuguese	English
Esq.	on left(-hand) side *(address)*
está	he/she/it is; you are
estação *f*	station; season
estação alta	high season
estação baixa	low season
estação de autocarros	bus station
estação de serviço	service station
estação do ano	season
estação do comboio	railway station
estacionamento *m*	parking
estacionar	to park *(car)*
Estados Unidos (EUA) *mpl*	United States
estar	to be
este/esta *m/f*	this
estes/estas *m/f*	these
estômago *m*	stomach
estrada *f*	road
estrada nacional (EN)	major road; national highway
estrada secundária	minor road
estrangeiro(a) *m/f*	foreigner
estranho(a)	strange
estudante *m/f*	student
etiqueta *f*	ticket; label; etiquette
eu	I
excesso de bagagem *m*	excess luggage; excess baggage
excursão *f*	excursion; tour
excursão guiada	guided tour
explicar	to explain

F

Portuguese	English
fácil	easy
fado *m*	traditional Portuguese song
falar	to speak
falta *f*	lack
falta de corrente	power cut
farmácia *f*	chemist's

farmácia permanente	duty chemist
farmácias de serviço	emergency chemists
fato *m*	suit *(man's)*
fato de banho	swimsuit
fato de treino	tracksuit
fatura *f*	invoice
favas *fpl*	broad beans
fazer	to do; to make
febre *f*	fever
febre dos fenos	hay fever
ter febre	to have a temperature
fechado(a)	closed
fechado Domingos e Feriados	closed Sundays and bank holidays
fechar	to shut; to close
feijão *m*	beans
feio(a)	awful; ugly
feira *f*	fair *(commercial)*; market
feliz	happy
feriado *m*	public holiday
feriado nacional	bank holiday
férias *fpl*	holidays
festa *f*	party *(celebration)*
fevereiro *m*	February
ficar	to stay; to be; to remain
ficar bem	to suit
fila *f*	row *(line)*; queue
filha *f*	daughter
filho *m*	son
fim *m*	end
fim de semana	weekend
flor *f*	flower
fogo *m*	fire
fome *f*	hunger
fora	out; outside
força *f*	power *(strength)*; force
forte	strong

fotografia *f*	photograph; print
fraco(a)	weak
frango *m*	chicken *(young and tender)*
freguês (freguesa) *m/f*	customer
frente *f*	front
em frente de	in front of; opposite
fresco(a)	fresh; cool; crisp
sirva fresco	serve chilled
frigorífico *m*	fridge
frio(a)	cold
fritar	to fry
frito(a)	fried
fruta *f*	fruit
fumadores *mpl*	smokers
para não fumadores	non-smoking *(compartment, etc.)*
fumar	to smoke
não fumar	no smoking
fumo *m*	smoke
funcionar	to work *(machine)*
não funciona	out of order *(sign)*
fundo(a)	deep

G

gabinete de provas *m*	changing room
galão *m*	large white coffee; gallon
galeria *f*	gallery
Gales: *o País de Gales*	Wales
galês (galesa)	Welsh
ganhar	to earn; to win
garagem *f*	garage
garantia *f*	guarantee
garoto *m*	boy; small white coffee
garrafa *f*	bottle
gás *m*	gas
a botija de gás	gas cylinder

gasóleo *m*	diesel
gasolina *f*	petrol
gasosa *f*	fizzy sweetened water
gastar	to spend
gelado *m*	ice cream; ice lolly
gelo *m*	ice
gente *f*	people
toda a gente	everybody
geral *adj*	general
em geral	generally
geralmente	usually
gerente *m/f*	manager
golfe *m*	golf
o taco de golfe	golf club *(stick)*
gordo(a)	fat
gorjeta *f*	tip *(to waiter, etc.)*
gostar de	to like
gosto *m*	taste
governo *m*	government
Grã-Bretanha *f*	Britain
grande	big; large; great
grávida	pregnant
gripe *f*	flu
grupo *m*	group; party *(group)*
grupo sanguíneo	blood group
guarda *m/f*	police officer
guarda-chuva *m*	umbrella
guardar	to keep; to watch over
guia *m/f*	guide
guisado *m*	stew

H

há	there is; there are
habitação *f*	residence; home
hoje	today
homem *m*	man

o wc dos homens	gents' toilet
hora *f*	hour; time *(by the clock)*
hora de ponta	rush hour
horário *m*	timetable
hortelã *f*	mint *(herb)*
hortelã-pimenta *f*	peppermint

I

ida *f*	visit; trip; single trip
ida e volta	return trip
idade *f*	age
identificação *f*	identification
idosos *mpl*	elderly people
igreja *f*	church
igual	equal; the same as
ilha *f*	island
impedido(a)	engaged *(phone)*
imperial *m*	draught beer
imposto *m*	tax; duty
impostos	duty; tax
impresso *m*	form *(to fill in)*
imprevisto(a)	unexpected
incêndio *m*	fire
incluído(a)	included
incomodar	to disturb
não incomodar	do not disturb
indicativo *m*	dialling code
infeção *f*	infection
inflamação *f*	inflammation
informação *f*	information
infração *f*	offence
Inglaterra *f*	England
inglês *m*	English *(language)*
inglês (inglesa)	English
inscrever	to register
insolação *f*	heatstroke; sunstroke

inteiro(a)	whole
interessante	interesting
intestinos *mpl*	bowels
intoxicação *f*	food poisoning
introduzir	to introduce; to insert
inverno *m*	winter
ir	to go
Irlanda *f*	Ireland
a Irlanda do Norte	Northern Ireland
irlandês (irlandesa)	Irish
irmã *f*	sister
irmão *m*	brother
IVA *m*	VAT

J

já	already; now
jamais	never
janeiro *m*	January
janela *f*	window
jantar *m*	dinner; evening meal
jardim *m*	garden
jogar	to play *(sport)*
jogo *m*	match; game; play
jornal *m*	newspaper
jovem	young
julho *m*	July
junho *m*	June
juntar	to join
junto	near

K

kg.	see **quilo(grama)**

L

lã *f*	wool
lado *m*	side

ao lado de	next to
ladrão (ladra) *m/f*	thief
lagosta *f*	lobster
lagostim *m*	Dublin Bay prawn
lampreia *f*	lamprey
laranja *f*	orange
o doce de laranja	marmalade
largo(a)	broad; loose *(clothes)*; wide
largura *f*	width
lavabo *m*	lavatory; toilet
lavandaria *f*	laundry
lavar	to wash *(clothes)*
legumes *mpl*	vegetables
lei *f*	law
leitão *m*	sucking pig
leite *m*	milk
com leite	white *(coffee)*
leite desnatado	skimmed milk
leite evaporado	evaporated milk
leite gordo	full-cream milk
leite magro	skimmed milk
leite meio-gordo	semi-skimmed milk
lembranças *fpl*	souvenirs
lençol *m*	sheet
lente *f*	lens
lentes de contacto	contact lenses
lento(a)	slow
ler	to read
levantar	to withdraw *(money)*; to lift
levantar-se	to stand up; get up *(from bed)*
levar	to take; to carry
leve	light *(not heavy)*
libra *f*	pound
libras esterlinas	pounds sterling
licença *f*	permit
ligação *f*	connection *(trains, etc.)*

ligado(a)	on *(engine, gas, etc.)*
limão *m*	lemon
limpar	to wipe; to clean
linha *f*	line; thread; platform *(railway)*
liquidação *f*	(clearance) sale
Lisboa (Lx)	Lisbon
lista *f*	list
lista de preços	price list
lista telefónica	telephone directory
litro *m*	litre
livraria *f*	bookshop
livre	free; vacant; for hire
livro *m*	book
lixo *m*	rubbish
loja *f*	shop
lombo *m*	loin *(cut of meat)*
longe	far
é longe?	is it far?
longo(a)	long
lotaria *f*	lottery
louro(a)	fair *(hair)*
lua-de-mel *f*	honeymoon
lugar *m*	seat *(theatre)*; place
lulas *fpl*	squid
luz *f*	light
Lx	see **Lisboa**

M

M.	underground *(metro)*
má	see **mau**
maçã *f*	apple
madeira *f*	wood
mãe *f*	mother
magro(a)	thin
maio *m*	May
maior	larger

M

Portuguese - English

a maior parte de	the majority of
mais	more
o/a mais	the most
mal *m*	wrong; evil
mala *f*	suitcase; bag; trunk
mal-estar *m*	discomfort
malpassado(a)	rare *(steak)*
mandar	to send; to order
manhã *f*	morning
manteiga *f*	butter
manter	to keep; to maintain
mapa *m*	map
mapa das estradas	road map
mapa das ruas	street plan
máquina *f*	machine
máquina fotográfica	camera
mar *m*	sea
maracujá *m*	passion fruit
março *m*	March
maré *f*	tide
maré alta	high tide
maré baixa	low tide
marido *m*	husband
marisco *m*	seafood; shellfish
mas	but
massa *f*	dough; pasta
matrícula *f*	number plate
mau (má)	bad; evil
me	me
média *f*	average
medicamento *m*	medicine
médico(a) *m/f*	doctor
médio(a)	medium
medusa *f*	jellyfish
meia *f*	stocking; half
meio *m*	middle
no meio de	in the middle of

meio(a)	half
meio-dia *m*	midday; noon
melhor	better
o/a melhor	the best
menina *f*	Miss; girl
menino *m*	boy
menor	smaller; minor *(under age)*
menos	least; less
mensagem *f*	message
mercado *m*	market
mercearia *f*	grocer's
mês *m*	month
mesa *f*	table
metade *f*	half
pela metade do preço	half-price
metro *m*	metre; underground *(rail)*
metropolitano *m*	tube *(underground)*
meu (minha)	my; mine
mexer	to move
não mexer	do not touch
mexilhão *m*	mussel
mil	thousand
mim	me
minha	see **meu**
mínimo(a)	minimum
moeda *f*	coin; currency
montanha *f*	mountain
morada *f*	address
morango *m*	strawberry
morar	to live; to reside
morder	to bite
fui mordido(a) por um cão	I was bitten by a dog
morrer	to die
mostrar	to show
motocicleta *f*	motorbike
motor *m*	engine; motor
motor de arranque	starter motor

motorista *m/f* driver
mudar to change
mudar-se to move house
muito very; much; quite *(rather)*
muitos(as) a lot (of); many; plenty (of)
mulher *f* female; woman; wife
multa *f* fine
mundo *m* world

N

nada nothing
nada a declarar nothing to declare
nadar to swim
namorado(a) *mf* boyfriend/girlfriend
não no; not
nascer to be born
nascimento *m* birth
nata *f* cream
Natal *m* Christmas
natureza *f* nature
neblina *f* mist
negativo(a) negative
negócios *mpl* business
nenhum(a) none
neve *f* snow
nevoeiro *m* fog
ninguém nobody
n.º see **número**
nocivo(a) harmful
nódoa *f* stain
noite *f* evening; night
à noite in the evening/at night
boa noite good evening/night
noivo(a) *adj* engaged *(to be married)*
m/f bride/groom; fiancé(e)

nome *m*	name
nome próprio	first name
normalmente	usually
nós	we; us
nosso(a)	our
notar	to notice
notícia *f*	piece of news
Nova Zelândia *f*	New Zealand
novembro *m*	November
novo(a)	new; young; recent
nublado(a)	dull *(weather)*; cloudy
número (n.º) *m*	number; size *(of clothes, shoes)*
nunca	never

O

o	the *(masculine)*
objeto *m*	object
objetos perdidos	lost property
obras *fpl*	roadworks; repairs
obrigado(a)	thank you
ocidental	western
oculista *m/f*	optician
óculos *mpl*	glasses
óculos de sol	sunglasses
ocupado(a)	engaged *(phone, toilet)*
oferecer	to offer; to give something
oferta *f*	offer; gift
olá	hello
óleo *m*	oil
óleo dos travões	brake fluid
olhar para/por	to look at/after
olho *m*	eye
onde	where
ontem	yesterday
ordem *f*	order
ou	or

ouro *m*	gold
de ouro	gold *(made of gold)*
outono *m*	autumn
outro(a)	other
outra vez	again
outubro *m*	October
ouvir	to hear; to listen (to)
ovo *m*	egg

P

padaria *f*	bakery
pagamento *m*	payment
pagamento a pronto	cash payment
pagar	to pay
página *f*	page
Páginas Amarelas®	Yellow Pages®
pago(a)	paid
pai *m*	father
pais	parents
país *m*	country
palácio *m*	palace
pane *f*	breakdown
pão *m*	bread; loaf
pão integral	wholemeal bread
pão torrado	toast
pão de trigo	wheat bread
papel *m*	paper
papel higiénico	toilet paper
papelaria *f*	stationer's
par *m*	pair; couple
para	for; towards; to
paragem *f*	stop *(for bus, etc.)*
parar	to stop
parque *m*	park
parquímetro *m*	parking meter
parte *f*	part

particular	private
partidas *fpl*	departures
partir	to break; to leave
a partir de...	from...
Páscoa *f*	Easter
passadeira *f*	zebra crossing
passado *m*	the past
passado(a): *bem passado(a)*	well done *(steak)*
passageiro *m*	passenger
passagem *f*	fare; crossing
passagem de nível	level-crossing
passagem de peões	pedestrian crossing
passagem proibida	no right of way
passagem subterrânea	underpass
passaporte *m*	passport
passar	to pass; to go by
passatempos *mpl*	hobbies
passe *m*	season ticket, pass
passe	go *(when crossing road)*; walk
passear	to go for a walk
passeio *m*	walk; pavement
pasta *f*	paste
pasta dentífrica	toothpaste
pastéis *mpl*	pastries
pastel *m*	pie; pastry *(cake)*
pastel folhado	puff pastry
pastelaria *f*	pastries; café; cake shop
pastilha *f*	pastille
pastilha elástica	chewing gum
pé *m*	foot
a pé	on foot
peça *f*	part; play
peças e acessórios	spares and accessories
pedir	to ask (for)
pedir alguma coisa	to ask for something
pedir emprestado(a)	to borrow
peixe *m*	fish

pensão *m*	guesthouse
pensão completa	full board
pensão residencial	boarding house
meia pensão	half board
pensar	to think
pepino *m*	cucumber
pepino de conserva	gherkin
pequeno(a)	little; small
pequeno-almoço	breakfast
pera *f*	pear
percebes *mpl*	rock barnacles
perder	to lose; to miss *(train, etc.)*
perdido(a)	lost
perdidos e achados	lost and found; lost property
pergunta *f*	question
perigo *m*	danger
perigo de incêndio	fire hazard
perigoso(a)	dangerous
permitir	to allow
perna *f*	leg
perto (de)	near
peru *m*	turkey
pesado(a)	heavy
pesar	to weigh
pesca *f*	fishing
pescada *f*	hake
pescar	to fish; to catch
peso *m*	weight
pêssego *m*	peach
pessoa *f*	person
pessoal *adj*	personal
pessoal *m*	staff; personnel
petiscos *mpl*	snacks; titbits
picada *f*	sting
uma picada de mosquito	a mosquito bite
picante	spicy

picar	to sting
pilha *f*	pile; battery *(for torch)*
pílula *f*	the pill
pimenta *f*	pepper
pimento *m*	pepper *(vegetable)*
pintar	to paint
pintura *f*	painting
pior	worse
pisca-pisca *m*	indicator *(on car)*
piscina *f*	swimming pool
piso *m*	floor; level; surface
piso escorregadio	slippery surface
planta *f*	plant; map
plateia *f*	stalls *(in theatre)*
pneu *m*	tyre
poder	to be able
poluição *f*	pollution
polvo *m*	octopus
pomada *f*	ointment
pomada para o calçado	shoe polish
ponte *f*	bridge
população *f*	population
por	by (through)
por aqui/por ali	this/that way
por hora	per hour
por pessoa	per person
pôr	to put
porção *f*	portion
porco *m*	pig; pork
por favor	please
porta *f*	door
a porta n.º ...	gate/door number...
portagem *f*	motorway toll
porteiro *m*	doorman
português *m*	Portuguese *(language)*
português (portuguesa)	Portuguese
posologia *f*	dose *(medicine)*

postal *m*	postcard
posto *m*	post; job
posto clínico	first aid post
posto de socorros	first aid centre
pouco(a)	little
pousada *f*	hotel; inn
povo *m*	people
praça *f*	square *(in town)*; market
praça de touros	bullring
praia *f*	beach; seaside
praticar	to practise
prato *m*	dish; plate; course of meal
prato da casa	speciality of the house
prato do dia	today's special
prazer *m*	pleasure
prazer em conhecê-lo	pleased to meet you
precisar de	to need
preciso(a): ***é preciso***	it is necessary
preço *m*	price
preencher	to fill in
prejuízo *m*	damage
prenda *f*	gift
preocupado(a)	worried
preparado(a)	ready
presente *m*	gift; present
preservativo *m*	condom
pressão *f*	pressure
pressão dos pneus	tyre pressure
preto(a)	black
primavera *f*	spring *(season)*
primeiro(a)	first
prioridade *f*	priority
prioridade à direita	give way to the right
produto *m*	product; proceeds
produtos alimentares	foodstuffs

professor(a) *m/f*	teacher
profissão *f*	occupation
profissão, idade, nome	occupation, age and name
profundo(a)	deep
proibido(a)	forbidden
proibida a entrada	no entry
proibido estacionar	no parking
proibido fumar	no smoking
proibida a paragem	no stopping
proibida a passagem	no access
proibido pisar a relva	do not walk on the grass
proibido tomar banho	no bathing
promoção *f*	special offer; promotion *(at work)*
pronto(a)	ready
proprietário(a) *m/f*	owner
provar	to taste; to try on
provisório(a)	temporary
próximo(a)	near; next
público *m*	audience; public
pulmão *m*	lung
puxar	to pull
puxe	pull *(sign)*

Q

quadro *m*	picture; painting
qual	which
quando	when
quanto(a)	how much
quantos(as)?	how many?
quanto tempo?	how long? *(time)*
quarta-feira *f*	Wednesday
quarto *m*	room; bedroom
quarto de banho	bathroom
quarto com duas camas	twin-bedded room
quarto de casal	double room

quarto individual	single room
quarto	fourth; quarter
que	what
o que é?	what is it?
quebrar	to break
queijada *f*	sweet cheese tartlet
queijo *m*	cheese
queimadura *f*	burn
queimadura do sol	sunburn *(painful)*
queixa *f*	complaint
quero apresentar uma queixa	I want to make a complaint
quem	who
quente *adj*	hot
querer	to want; to wish
quilo(grama) (kg.) *m*	kilo
quilómetro *m*	kilometre
quinta-feira *f*	Thursday
quiosque *m*	kiosk; newsstand
quotidiano(a)	daily

R

R.	see **rua**
radiografia *f*	X-ray
rapariga *f*	girl
rapaz *m*	boy
rápido *m*	express *(train)*
rápido(a)	fast
rato *m*	mouse
rebuçado *m*	boiled sweet
recado *m*	message
dar um recado	to give a message
receber	to receive
receção *f*	reception
receita *f*	recipe
receita médica	prescription
recibo *m*	receipt

Portuguese	English
reclamação *f*	protest; official complaint
recolher	to collect
recolha de bagagem	baggage reclaim
recompensa *f*	reward
reconhecer	to recognize
recordação *f*	souvenir
reembolsar	to reimburse
refeição *f*	meal
reformado(a) *m/f*	pensioner
região *f*	area (region)
registar	to register
regulamentos *mpl*	regulations
Reino Unido *m*	United Kingdom
relógio *m*	watch; clock
relva *f*	grass
não pisar a relva	keep off the grass
remédio *m*	medicine; remedy
reparar	to fix; to repair
repetir	to repeat
rés do chão (R/C) *m*	ground floor
reservar	to book; to reserve
residência *f*	boarding house; residence
responder	to answer; to reply
resposta *f*	answer
reunião *f*	meeting
revista *f*	magazine
rins *mpl*	kidneys
rio *m*	river
rodovia *f*	highway
roteiro *m*	guidebook
roubar	to steal; to rob
roupa *f*	clothes
roupa de cama	bedding
roupa interior	underwear
rua (R.) *f*	street
rubéola *f*	German measles
ruído *m*	noise

S

S.	see **São**
sábado *m*	Saturday
saber	to know *(fact)*
sabonete *m*	toilet soap
saco *m*	bag; handbag
saia *f*	skirt
saída *f*	exit; way out
saídas	departures
sair	to go out; to come out
sal *m*	salt
sala *f*	room
sala de chá	tea room; café
sala de embarque	departure lounge
sala de espera	waiting room
sala de estar	living room; lounge
sala de jantar	dining room
salada *f*	salad
salão *m*	hall *(for concerts, etc.)*
salário *m*	wage; salary
saldo *m*	sale
salgado(a)	salty; savoury
salmão *m*	salmon
salpicão *m*	spicy sausage
salsa *f*	parsley
salsicha *f*	sausage
salsicharia *f*	delicatessen
salteado(a) sandes *f*	sautéed sandwich
sanduíche *m*	sandwich
sangue *m*	blood
sanitários *mpl*	toilets
Santo(a) (Sto./Sta.) *m/f*	Saint
São (S.) *m*	Saint
sapataria *f*	shoe shop
sapateira *f*	type of crab
sapato *m*	shoe

sarampo *m*	measles
sardinha *f*	sardine
satisfeito(a)	happy; satisfied
saúde *f*	health
saúde!	cheers!
se	if; whether
se faz favor (SFF)	please
sé *f*	cathedral
secar	to dry; to drain *(tank)*
seco(a)	dry
secretária *f*	desk
secretário(a) *m/f*	secretary
século *m*	century
sede *f*	thirst
ter sede	to be thirsty
seguir	to follow
seguir pela direita	keep to your right
seguir pela esquerda	keep to your left
segunda-feira *f*	Monday
segundo *m*	second *(time)*
segundo(a)	second
segundo andar	second floor
de segunda classe	second-class
em segunda mão	second-hand
segurança *f*	safety
segurar	to hold
seguro *m*	insurance
seguro contra terceiros	third party insurance
seguro contra todos os riscos	comprehensive insurance
seguro de viagem	travel insurance
seguro(a)	safe; reliable
seio *m*	breast
selo *m*	stamp
sem	without
semáforos *mpl*	traffic lights
semana *f*	week

para a semana	next week
na semana passada	last week
por semana	weekly *(rate, etc.)*
semanal	weekly
senhor *m*	sir; gentleman; you
Senhor	Mr
senhora *f*	lady; madam; you
Senhora	Mrs, Ms
senhorio(a) *m/f*	landlord/lady
sentar-se	to sit (down)
sentido *m*	sense; meaning
sentido único	one-way street
sentir	to feel
ser	to be
serviço *m*	service; cover charge
serviço de quartos	room service
seriviço de urgência	accident and emergency
serviço (não) incluído	service (not) included
serviço permanente	24-hour service
servir	to serve
setembro *m*	September
seu (sua)	his; her; your
sexta-feira *f*	Friday
SFF	see **se faz favor**
significar	to mean
sim	yes
simpático(a)	nice; friendly
sinal *m*	signal; deposit *(part payment)*
sinal de impedido	engaged tone
sinal de marcação	dialling tone
sinal de trânsito	road sign
sítio *m*	place; spot
situado(a)	situated
só	only; alone
sobre	over; on top of
sobre o mar	overlooking the sea

sobrecarga *f*	excess load; surcharge
sobremesa *f*	dessert
sócio *m*	member; partner
socorro *m*	help; assistance
socorro 112	emergency service 112
sogro(a) *m/f*	father-in-law/mother-in-law
sol *m*	sun
solteiro(a)	single *(not married)*
som *m*	sound
soma *f*	amount *(sum)*
sopa *f*	soup
sorte *f*	luck; fortune
boa sorte	good luck
sorvete *m*	water ice; sorbet
sua	see **seu**
subir	to go up
suficiente	enough
sujo(a)	dirty
sumo *m*	juice
supermercado *m*	supermarket
surdo(a)	deaf

T

tabacaria *f*	tobacconist's; newsagent
tabaco *m*	tobacco
tabela *f*	list; table
taberna *f*	tavern
talheres *mpl*	cutlery
talho *m*	butcher's
talvez	perhaps
tamanho *m*	size
também	also; too
tamboril *m*	monkfish
tanto(a)	so much
tão	so
isto é tão bonito	this is so beautiful

T

Portuguese - English

tarde *f*	afternoon
boa tarde	good afternoon
tarde *adv*	late (in the day)
tarifa *f*	charge; rate
tarifas de portagem	toll charges
tasca *f*	tavern; wine bar; restaurant
taxa *f*	fee; rate
taxa de juro	interest rate
taxa normal	peak-time rate
taxa reduzida	off-peak rate
teatro *m*	theatre
telecomandado(a)	remote-controlled
teleférico *m*	cable car
telefonista *m/f*	operator
televisão *f*	television
tempero *m*	dressing *(for salad)*; seasoning
tempestade *f*	storm
tempo *m*	weather; time *(duration)*
tempo inteiro	full-time
tempo parcial	part-time
temporada *f*	season
temporário(a)	temporary
tensão *f*	tension
tensão arterial alta/baixa	high/low blood pressure
tentar	to try
ter	to have
terça-feira *f*	Tuesday
terceiro(a)	third
para a terceira idade	for the elderly
termas *fpl*	spa
terra *f*	earth; ground
terramoto *m*	earthquake
tesoura *f*	scissors
tinturaria *f*	dry-cleaner's
tipo *m*	sort; kind
tirar	to remove; to take out

tiro *m* shot
toalha *f* towel
tocar to touch; to ring; to play
tocar piano to play the piano
todo(a) all; the whole
toda a gente everyone
todas as coisas everything
em toda a parte everywhere
tomar to take
tomar banho to bathe; to have a bath
tomar antes de se deitar take at bedtime
tomar em jejum take on an empty stomach
tomar ... vezes ao dia take ... times a day
toranja *f* grapefruit
torcer to twist; to turn
torrada *f* toast
torre *f* tower
tosse *f* cough
tosta *f* toasted sandwich
tosta de queijo toasted cheese sandwich
totoloto *m* lottery
toucinho *m* bacon
tourada *f* bullfight
touro *m* bull
trabalhar to work *(person)*
trabalho *m* work
trabalhos na estrada roadworks
tradução *f* translation
traduzir to translate
tráfego *m* traffic
tranquilo(a) calm; quiet
transferir to transfer
trânsito *m* traffic
trânsito condicionado restricted traffic
trânsito proibido no entry
transtorno *m* upset; inconvenience

trás: ***para trás***	backwards
no banco de trás	on the back seat *(car)*
a parte de trás	the back
tratamento *m*	treatment
tratar de	to treat; to deal with
travar	to brake
trazer	to bring; to carry
triângulo *m*	warning triangle
trigo *m*	wheat
triste	sad
trocar	to exchange; to change
troco *m*	change *(money)*
trocos	small change
truta *f*	trout
tu	you *(informal)*
tubo *m*	exhaust pipe; tube; hose
tudo	everything; all

U

ultimamente	lately; recently
último(a)	last; latest
ultrapassar	to overtake; to pass
um(a)	a; an; one
único(a)	single; unique
unidade *f*	unit *(hi-fi, etc.)*; unity
unir	to join
usado(a)	used *(car, etc.)*
usar	to use; to wear
útil	useful
utilização *f*	use
utilizar	to use
uva *f*	grape

V

vaca *f*	cow
vacina *f*	vaccination
vagão-restaurante *m*	buffet car
vagas *fpl*	vacancies
valer	to be worth
válido(a)	valid
válido(a) até...	valid until...
valor *m*	value
variado(a)	assorted
varicela *f*	chickenpox
vários(as)	several
vazio(a)	empty
velho(a)	old
velocidade *f*	gear; speed
velocidade limitada	speed limit in force
vencimento *m*	wage; due date
venda *f*	sale *(in general)*
venda proibida	not for public sale
vendas e reparações	sales and repairs
vender	to sell
vende-se	for sale
vento *m*	wind
ver	to see; to look at
verão *m*	summer
verdade *f*	truth
não é verdade?	wouldn't you agree?
verdadeiro(a)	true
verde	green
verificar	to check
vermelho(a)	red
véspera *f*	the day before; the eve
vestiário *m*	cloakroom; changing room
vestido *m*	dress
vestir	to dress; to wear
vestir-se	to get dressed
veterinário(a) *m/f*	vet

vez *f*	time; turn
às vezes	occasionally; sometimes
uma vez	once
duas vezes	twice
muitas vezes	often
é a sua vez	it's your turn
via *f*	road, lane
via aérea	by air mail
via nasal	to be inhaled
via oral	orally
viaduto *m*	viaduct; flyover
viagem *f*	trip; journey
viagem de negócios	business trip
viajar	to travel
vida *f*	life
vidros *mpl*	glassware
vila *f*	small town
vindima *f*	harvest *(of grapes)*
vinho *m*	wine
vir	to come
virar	to turn
vire à direita	turn right
vire à esquerda	turn left
visitar	to visit
vista *f*	view
com linda vista	with a beautiful view
visto *m*	visa
vitela *f*	veal
vivenda *f*	house; villa
viver	to live
vivo(a)	alive
vizinho(a) *m/f*	neighbour
você(s)	you
volta *f*	turn
à volta (de)	about
em volta (de)	around
dar uma volta	to go for a short walk/ride

voltar	to return *(go/come back)*
volto já	I'll be back in a minute
voo *m*	flight
voo fretado	charter flight
voo normal	scheduled flight
vos	you; to you
vós	you
vosso	your, yours

W

windsurf *m*	windsurfing

X

xadrez *m*	chess
xarope *m*	syrup
xarope para a tosse	cough syrup
xerez *m*	sherry

Z

zona *f*	zone
zona de banhos	swimming area
zona interdita	no thoroughfare